How To
Draw
Cartoons
and
Caricatures

How To Draw Cartoons and Caricatures

by

Mark Linley

A HOW TO BOOK

ROBINSON

ROBINSON

First published in Great Britain in 1999 under the title
How to Cartoon or Caricature Anyone.
This edition published in Great Britain in 2013 by Robinson

A CIP catalogue record for this book is available from the British Library.

ISBN: 978-0-7160-2351-7

Printed and bound in Great Britain by Clays Ltd, Elcograf S.p.A.

Papers used by Robinson are from well-managed forests
and other responsible sources

Robinson
An imprint of
Little, Brown Book Group
Carmelite House
50 Victoria Embankment
London EC4Y 0DZ

An Hachette UK Company
www.hachette.co.uk

www.littlebrown.co.uk

How To Books are published by Robinson, an imprint of Little, Brown Book Group.
We welcome proposals from authors who have first-hand experience of their subjects.
Please set out the aims of your book, its target market and its suggested contents in an
email to Nikki.Read@howtobooks.co.uk

Dedication

To all my friends, bless them.

Acknowledgements

Drawings by Pat Finn: Figures 77, 78 and 79.
Drawings by John Ball:
Figures 206, 210, 212, 217, 219, 221, 223, and 248.
Drawings by Colin Henderson:
Figures 122, 171, 174, 175, 176, 177, 178, 180, 196, 199, 202, 203, 208, 209, 222, 228, 229, 230, 231, 238, 242.

All the other pictures are by the author.

Contents

1

Raise A Smile, Prompt A Laugh

Welcome to my new cartoon and caricature book. The fact that you want to draw cartoons makes you quite special. Why? Because you belong to a group of people who have the ability to raise a smile or prompt a laugh in others. In our modern stressful world humour is golden. There just isn't enough to go round. The best medicine in the world is laughter.

One of the many joys of being a cartoonist is knowing that someone somewhere has had their day brightened by a tiny bit of magic which you have created. You are embarking on a worthwhile project, chum. I shall help you to do your job and to enjoy it.

What to aim for
You already know that your first aim is to make people smile if not explode with a belly-laugh of huge proportions or collapse in a helpless shrieking heap!

Your next target is to produce cartoon drawings which are funny. How do you do this? Read on, then try to draw all the assignments in this book. By doing the exercises you will quickly improve your observation and drawing skills. You will widen the range of your drawing ability and become a pretty good all-round artist. Isn't that good news?

You will find almost all drawings in this book have help lines. No matter how raw a talent you have or how little

1. You are very special.

sketching experience has come your way you will quickly pick up the essential parts of being a good cartoonist. You should also learn how to use your imagination which is a vital quality needed by all artists, writers and creative people. You can learn many tricks of the trade from these pages. Above all aim to *enjoy* learning and practising as much as I love teaching.

Your shopping list for starters
The cost of art materials which you will need is relatively small; much less than the expense of most other hobbies or pastimes. While it always pays to shop around do not be tempted to buy the

cheapest products as these might work against you.

You will need good quality paper. You should buy typing or computer paper 85 or 90 g/m in weight. This is best purchased in reams (500) sheets. This may sound like a lot of paper but don't worry you can fill ten pieces with cartoons in less than 20 minutes!

To illustrate my books I use black fibre-tipped drawing pens size 01 and 07. See figure 2 to get an idea of how different pens give a different line thickness. For some cartoons I might use an artist's dip pen along with a bottle of black drawing ink. A dip pen is useful if you want variations in line. I have also used

2. **Different pens for different lines.**

calligraphy pens. Don't be afraid to try out many different sorts and brands of pen. If possible go for pens which are colour fast or waterproof, but to begin with any old black pen which produces a clean line would do. We each have our favourite pens.

Right, that's your main weapon sorted out. You will also need a 2B drawing pencil. This is a fairly soft pencil. Along with this buy a medium hard eraser and a craft knife or blade with which to sharpen your pencils.

A small watercolour paint brush size 4 or 5 would come in handy for blocking in large areas such as black hair, black clothes and so on. A small bottle of black drawing ink should keep you going for months and months. A little bottle of Process White is a good thing to have. This is thick white paint which is useful for correcting small mistakes.

Later on when you have gained experience you may want to have your own lay figure, but I will mention more about these drawing aids in Chapter 5.

Your mind is a personal computer!
To be successful in most projects you have to think positively. This can be very easy to do. Always think and say that you CAN learn to do. Never ever think that you can't; that's negative. Why does positive thinking work like magic? Because in your brain is a sub-conscious mind which is often faster and smarter than the most up-to-date computer. In fact, it is a super personal computer. How do you program this essential tool? Simply by the way you think. If, for example, you think that you can do something, then you will. Your computer likes to receive messages as pictures so you should send one of yourself achieving exactly what you want. Isn't that simple?

Your computer will also work just as fast against you if you think a negative thought which it also takes as an instruction. Mind how you think, chum.

It could be that you come across a problem which you feel you cannot solve. Ninety-nine out of every hundred people faced with this situation immediately think "I can't" when what they really mean is "I don't know how to".

The hardest part of becoming positive about all things in your life is to abandon all negative thoughts. For some folk this is tough because they have tended to think negatively all their lives. But this should not happen to you. You have me to help you along the right path. Don't mind me being a rather bossy teacher or you might get your hands smacked!

Start with doodles
Now that your self-confidence has risen quicker than a bad dose of wind you are ready to start.

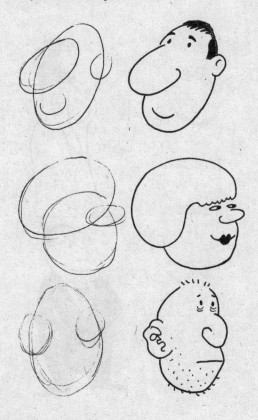

3. **Doodle ovals, then turn them into faces.**

Study as many cartoons as you can then make a page or two of pencil doodles based on those which appeal most to you. Sketch oval face shapes and figures in pencil. See figures 3 and 4 as examples. Copy these cartoons.

Doodles can produce the most surprising creations. I did a rough doodle of a girl. She was pretty but her looks, it seemed to me, were off-set by the pair of huge boots she wore. My doodle was changed from a rough sketch into a cartoon creation which was named Super Doodle. She appeared in an

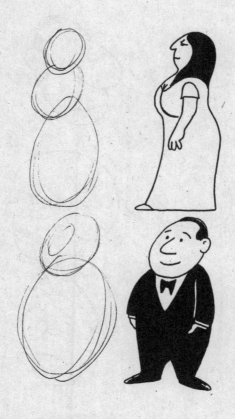

4. Oval doodles can produce figures.

earlier book of mine but has now been updated. You can follow her adventures from figure 5.

Assignments
1. Draw a page of funny faces.
2. Have a go at drawing one cartoon male and female figure.
3. Try to create something funny from a doodle.

5.   Hello, Super Doodle!

2

Simply Easy

In this chapter I will show you how to set about drawing faces. You can start with simple sketches of different face types. Once you have mastered this art you can then move on to more advanced exercises in following chapters.

It is important to be able to sketch faces quickly because they are the first thing a reader looks at. If your cartoon face looks like a squashed bread pudding your reader won't bother to look at anything else. If, on the other hand, you can come up with a face which has instant appeal and seems funny you are well on your way to success.

Try to be simple
Look at figure 6 to see how just a few lines can produce a nice cartoon face. The top sketch shows how to start this drawing. The ink sketch reveals how two simple lines accurately depict a hair style. Notice how an upturned top lip can suggest a smile. It's small things like this that you have to learn as you go. Don't worry about it. I shall gently guide you there.

Always begin by using a 2B pencil to plan the head roughly. When you are satisfied with your efforts, go over the lines with a pen. Then erase the pencil marks. This simple system works every time. Always draw larger than the printed illustration. Leave plenty of space above your sketch because you will be putting in word or thought balloons. Try out this system by drawing your version of the female face in figure 6.

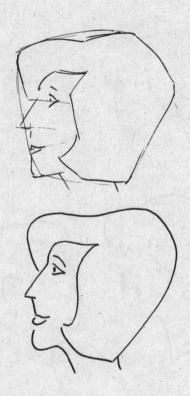

6. Just a few lines.

Notice that most cartoon faces are roughly based on ovals or circles. So it's a good idea to play about with your pencil first; to put down a series of shapes which appeal to you, ready to turn into faces. You then mark in where you want the mouth, eyes, ears, nose and hair. When you get used to doing this routine you should find that it takes only seconds to create cartoon characters. Your first rough pencil sketch is most important. On this you succeed or fail. But, now you are thinking positively, you won't have any problems. Will you?

Figure 7, again of few lines, depicts a boy and girl cartoon. See how the rough pencil sketches are easy to draw. To keep

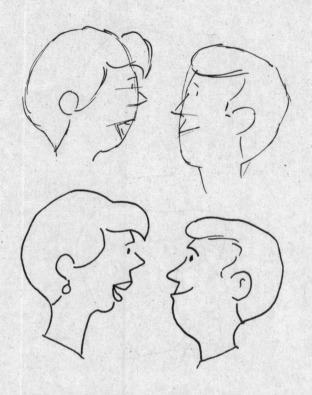

7. Your first rough sketch is the start.

your style simple remember to leave out as many lines as you can. In the examples in figure 7 notice which small lines have been left out and which ones have been used. Figure 8 is similar but different! See how a little dot can be used to suggest an eye.

The faces used for figure 9 have one tiny difference from the previous illustrations. I have added eyelids. That's all but see how one small item can make a more advanced face.

Now draw all the faces in figures 7, 8 and 9. If your pencil

18

8. Similar, but different!

roughs turn into pen drawings anything like mine give yourself a big pat on the back. Not too hard mind, you have dozens of other drawings to do!

Use help lines
When you sketch a cartoon face try to remember that the human face is rather egg-shaped. Look at the top rough sketches used in figure 10. See how I have put dotted lines in to show the shape of the face, where the eyes and mouth go. Why should you do this? Because it helps you to get everything right before you begin your masterpiece. And because I say so!

These faces have eyes which have been drawn as small

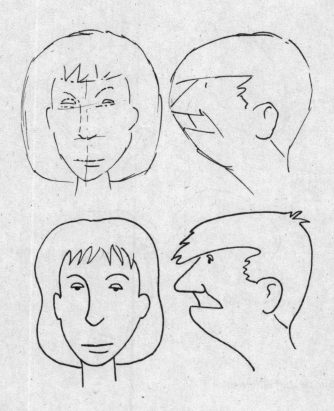

9. Add an eyelid.

circles with pupils then added in. Where the pupils are put needs thinking about. The two characters are glancing at each other. See how the eyes suggest this. Notice also how a straight-line mouth suggests a neutral or doubtful state of mind. The two are weighing each other up. This simple cartoon is to show you how two items, eyes and mouth, can suggest the mood of a cartoon person.

Thought and word balloons
In figure 10 you will see that I have expressed the characters' thoughts by using a single thought balloon. Word and thought

10. Use help lines in your roughs.

balloons are easy to draw. They are very useful devices. You can start using them from here on. You simply enclose the words or sounds in a cloud-like shape. The best way to do this is first to pencil in a straight line for the words. Write in the caption then enclose it. This is much easier than drawing a balloon, then trying to cram in the words afterwards. It's one of many tricks of our trade!

Figure 11 was drawn to show you how just the mouth line can depict mood. This important line curves upwards for happiness and down for gloom, or anger. If, like me, you decide to adopt just dots for your cartoon characters' eyes, then stick to this for general cartoons, but be sure to use the mouth to obtain the result you want. Another feature to help

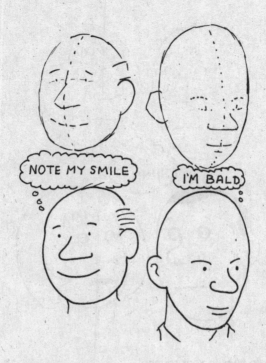

11. Mouth lines can depict moods.

you is the eyebrows. See figure 12. Eyebrows tend to rise or arch for happy moods. They arrow down for anger. You can always use a mirror to act out the moods. Then you just note what your own features do. Anyone watching you do this assumes that you're mad. This may help you to build up a suitable persona. Being rather dotty has been a huge advantage to me. I don't have to pretend. It's my natural state!

Figure 13 again reveals how the same features can be used to show moods. All these examples use mouth, eyes and eyebrows to show mood. The top cartoon character is yelling. I have used a word balloon to enclose the words. This differs from a thought balloon by having a continuous line round the

12. Mouth, eyes and eyebrows.

words. When you get the hang of using these tricks you are then in command of all your little people. Let the power go to your head. It's occasionally good for you!

Now have a go at quickly drawing figures 10, 11, 12 and 13. With a little practice a rough pencil sketch of a face takes around ten seconds to draw and another twelve to ink in. You can have double this time for your first efforts. I'm a big softie!

The young and the old
Babies have large round heads, so are easy to draw as cartoons, but difficult to obtain a likeness of for a serious portrait. Figure 14 shows a frontal view and a profile of babies. The mouth is exaggerated in the illustration of a little

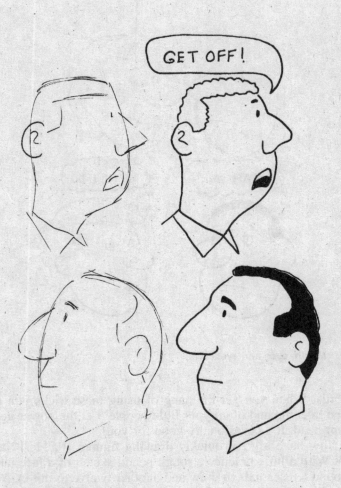

13.   A word balloon.

monster crying. Draw your version of these small victims.
Figure 15 moves on to early teenage. Notice, again, how help
lines make the drawing easy. The boy has a heart-shaped face.
The girl is oval-faced. You should have no problems with
these.

14. Note the round head shapes.

The ancient are easy
When we get old we become rather like an old car. Parts need replacing, body work putting right plus a darn good servicing. For a cartoonist, however, the more wrinkles the better. Figure 16 was drawn from two elderly gentlemen. Notice the glasses, shortage of hair and wrinkles. Draw your cartoons of these old fellows. They seem to be reflecting on life, living in the past or wondering what is for supper. Think out a word or thought balloon for each.

The really ancient are super to draw as cartoons, poor things, because of all the lines, bags, wrinkles and huge noses and ears.

15. Young teenagers' thoughts!

If you don't already know, let me inform you that nose and ears continue to grow in old age whilst the rest of the equipment shrinks. Now isn't that something to look forward to?

Figure 17 of an elderly couple, aged around a hundred, uses all the features I've just mentioned but more so. Have a shot at

16. Facial lines help you.

drawing them. What are they thinking about? Come up with something funny then enclose your witty gems inside thought balloons. Keep your masterpieces as a warning of things to come!

Assignments
1. Invent a cartoon face then draw it with as few lines as possible.

17. The wrinklies are lovely models.

2. Draw an angry girl using just the mouth and eyebrows to show her mood. Use a thought balloon to express what she thinks.
3. Depict a teenager smiling at a grumpy old person. Use a word or thought balloon to tell readers what each character's mood is.

18. Splat!

3

More Fun With Faces

You should be ready now to move on a bit. The faces in this chapter, taken from life, show some of the many face types we have in our multi-cultured society. There will never be a shortage of models. There's too many of us on this crowded planet but what an advantage this is for us cartoonists. Some of the examples are pretty life-like whilst others are pure cartoons but still based on real people spotted by the author.

Be multi-cultural

Almost every city in the UK, Europe and many other countries is now multi-cultured. Wherever you go you will see people who represent scores of nationalities. It's a rich source of cartoon faces. The world now comes to you.

In this section you can practise drawing some of the many races who now combine into nations.

Figure 19 shows two faces taken from city life. See how shading has been applied, how hair styles are depicted. Notice how accurate the first rough pencil sketches are. Draw your versions of these faces. Allow yourself plenty of room to put in word or thought balloons. What is the girl laughing about? What has made the man grin? Think out something really wild and funny.

Move on to figures 20 and 21. Notice the hatted character (top in figure 21); this face was based on that of a famous

19. Collect every kind of face.

20. More types.

21. Try hat and moustache, or dog collar.

French actor. The West Indian face below is from life. Both are fairly life-like. You can stretch or simplify your sketches of these faces. Don't forget the word or thought balloons. These are created as an exercise to train you to think out funny one-liners which are an essential part of becoming a good cartoonist. Treat it as fun. Then it will be.

Figures 22, 23 and 24 on the following pages, illustrate more nationalities taken from life. Look carefully at them. Decide which are life-like and which have been exaggerated. Do not slavishly copy what I have drawn; use a bit of yourself in your work then you will quickly develop your own unique style.

Collect faces

A good way of helping yourself to become a good artist is to go out and draw faces. I am sure that you have already realised this. The difficult part, for a beginner, is to have the courage to do this. Do not be afraid. Almost everyone is pleased to be drawn as a cartoon. If, however, you are nervous just force

22. Different races are, well, different!

23. Every nationality has its own characteristics.

yourself into the great outdoors then hide away so that your victims cannot easily see what you are up to. Very often this is the best way because some folk tend to become camera conscious if they know that they are being drawn. There is more about lurking in Chapter 6.

Pay attention to the many different ethnic types. Be able to draw anyone of any nationality. Collect different types by popping them down as rough sketches in your sketch pad. You can then work these up into finished drawings at your leisure. Keep your eyes open and pencil ready when you go out.

When you were young you might have added glasses on to images in newspapers or magazines. I did. It was a start. Whilst collecting faces you will notice that some of your victims wear a hat, may have a beard and so on. Try adding on

24. Let the World come to you!

33

a few of these items just for practice. If you are unable to get about easily, another way forward is to cartoon faces from newspapers, magazines or television. "Where there is a will, there is a way", is a very true old saying.

Imagination

Imagination is the ability to see mental pictures. Make up things, in other words. Some people have more imagination than others but it is a faculty which can be developed and trained. For a cartoonist it is vital.

Recently I attended a course (non-artistic) in London and popped down sketches of fellow students – and the tutor – as I listened to many hours of talks. One exercise given to us students was to act or think out a story as a five year old. This was great fun to do. My five year old wanted to rob a bank, steal a posh car or sell drugs at his infant school. He also had a drink problem. Instead of hot milk at night he demanded a cup of Sherry followed by a Vodka chaser. His morning Wheaty Bits were served in mulled red wine. To escape unhappiness the little beast drew cartoons. I showed the 60 strong group his cartoon of the tutor. The group laughed when they heard my yarn and applauded. This true story is mentioned because it shows how *imagination* and a sense of humour can brighten our lives.

If you think that you have poor imagination, try out your cartoon brain by seeing what is around you. For example look at a table set for tea. What about making the teapot into a little cartoon with eyes, nose (spout) and a mouth. It can talk. So can cups, spoons and plates. What can they say or think?

Walk round a garden. See flowers as small faces. Some smile, some are glum, all talk, think, express opinions. Let your *imagination* run riot. It's great fun. Try it.

Try different eyes

Back to work now. Look back at figure 24 to see how eyes have been treated. The top character has dots for eyes. The

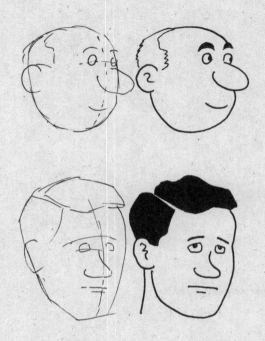

25. Let the eyes have it!

eyes in the middle head are circles. The character at the bottom of the page wears glasses. Re-draw all these cartoons then put in thought balloons to help sum up their mood.

Figures 25, 26 and 27 illustrate other ways of drawing eyes. Notice the shape of them. Draw your version of my faces. Think out balloons for your inventions.

Glamour pusses
Beautiful faces are used in cartoons. Some can be rather life-like. This kind (fig 28) are used to sell products. Notice that the eyes are pretty true to life. Face shapes have been slightly exaggerated, hair styles simplified and mouths stretched a bit. Your pencil roughs should be as good as you

26. Another way with eyes.

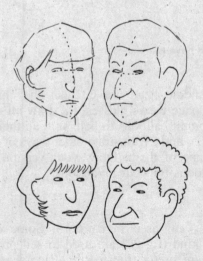

27. What are they thinking?

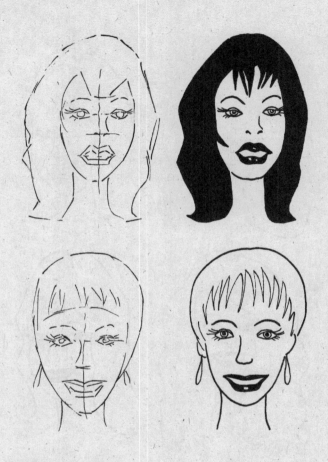

28. Glamour puss.

can draw them for these faces before you ink them in. What can the girls be thinking? That's up to you. Figure 29 is a similar exercise for you.

I deliberately turned glamour girls into cartoons for figure 30. Eyes, mouths and faces were exaggerated. The hair styles are drawn with few lines. This type of face is the sort to use in everyday pocket cartoons. There will be more about these later

29. Hair exaggerated a bit.

in this book. Draw your faces then put in word or thought balloons.

Assignments
1. From life draw a male and female face type.

30. Glamour stretched further than it will go?

31. Vengeance threatened!

2. See if you can cartoon an Asian face.
3. Make a cartoon from a newspaper picture.

4

Hands And Feet

Before you move on to drawing whole cartoon figures you should have a little practice on sketching hands and feet. Most beginners tend to draw these appendages much too small. Cartoonists exaggerate these features. You can see many examples in newspapers and magazines. If you want to draw huge feet that is fine. Hands can have just three fingers or be life-like. It's up to you.

Be handy with hands

You can draw fingers like stubby sausages or rather like a bunch of bananas. Always start by drafting out a pencil rough. A helpful friend would be useful as a model for you. Failing that you can always use your own hands to draw from. To do this use a mirror. Another tip is to notice how people use their hands. Drawing from life is always the best way forward. Study your victims.

Look at the cartoon hands drawn for figure 32. See how the rough sketches have been constructed. You will soon get the hang of drawing hands by drawing hands. Figure 33 is of more hands in different positions. Notice that you can leave out nails if you wish to. You can also get away with just using three fingers and a thumb. I prefer to draw the whole thing but that's my choice. Draw a page or two of hands based on those you have just studied.

The hands of ladies, of course, are usually quite different

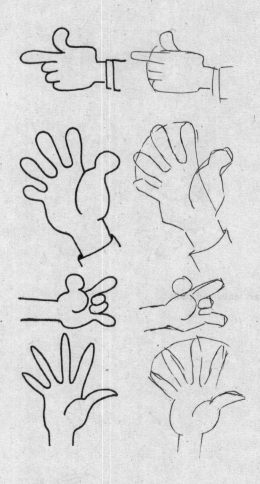

32. Draw a pencil rough first.

from those of men. Female hands tend to be much slimmer and smooth with tapering fingers. Figure 34 is of such hands. Notice the action lines used to indicate movement. Draw your version of these hands.

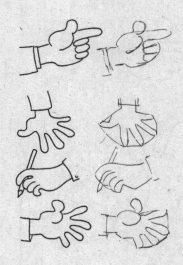

33. You can leave out nails.

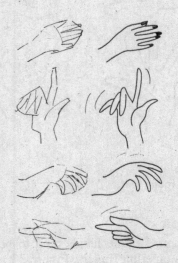

34. Ladies' hands.

Big feet

I am sure that you must have noticed how most cartoonists put huge feet on their cartoon creations. You can do the same. In fact, cartoon characters with tiny feet seem somehow wrong. Play about with your pencil until you come up with footwear you like on your creations.

It's a good idea to keep a record of modern shoes and other footwear, then you can easily refer to the notes if you are stuck with a sketch and do not quite remember what certain gear looks like. The footwear illustrating figure 35 was drawn from a catalogue. Sketching fairly accurate records of footwear will improve your observation and give you a feel for foot shapes and sizes.

35. Keep notes of footwear.

For most general cartoon characters footwear is very simply drawn but there are times when more life-like illustrations are needed – for cartoon characters used to advertise a product for example. Copy the designs in figure 35 then move on to figure 36 which shows footwear exaggerated for use in cartoons.

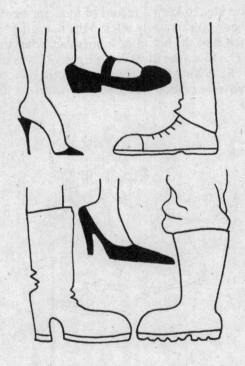

36. Shoes and boots exaggerated.

Notice that the drawings do resemble the real thing although they have been slightly exaggerated. Draw similar footwear but first pop down a pencil rough.

The footwear in figure 37 has also been exaggerated. You may have noticed that in cartoons featuring elegant ladies the

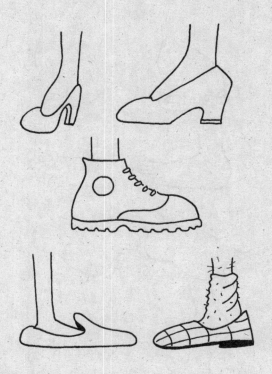

37. Cartoons based on the real thing.

artist will usually clad them in high-heeled shoes. A tramp, on the other hand, should be wearing battered boots tied with string. His toes could poke out. The elderly might be seen to wear decrepit slippers similar to those drawn for figure 37. See how painfully thin legs or wrinkled socks help to suggest age. See if you can stretch the studies even further.

Bare feet
Sometimes it is necessary to draw a cartoon figure who has bare feet. Just as it's useful to keep notes on footwear it is helpful to make records of naked feet drawn as cartoons. You

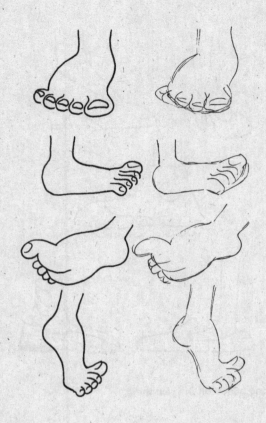

38. Cartoon feet.

can use a mirror to sketch your own hooves, or get a bit of help from your friends. Accurate anatomical drawings are not required. Keep your sketch simple. Exaggerate the big toe, make the foot more rounded, longer or whatever shape you fancy but remember – your readers must recognise them as feet!

Figure 38 will give you an idea of cartoon feet and also the first pencil roughs. See if you can draw a page of feet but in different positions from those shown.

Assignments

1. Draw the legs and footwear of a policeman.
2. Invent a cartoon teenager who is wearing trainers.
3. Draw a high-heeled shoe from the front then from the side.

39. Anticipation . . .

5

Lay It On

Now you should be ready to start figure drawing for your cartoons. A most useful aid to figure drawing is a little manikin called a lay figure. These are made of wood. They have jointed limbs which allow them to be moved into any normal position common to us humans. The one I use has a small nose (modelling clay) added on, plus drawn-in eyes and mouth. It is a very useful teaching aid quite apart from helping me to knock out cartoons.

If you are unable to get about or have no relatives or friends to pose or you are in a hurry to get things done (like me) a lay figure could be the answer to your problem.

Lay figures can be purchased for a few pounds. If you want one shop around for it. Some art stores charge quite a lot for them but there are bargain shops which stock less expensive ones.

How to use a lay figure
Figure 40 will show you what my lay figure looks like. It is 32 cm high. There are lay figures which are either larger or smaller than this. You have a choice. Don't go in for a life-sized one. It might trigger nightmares for you!

See how the lay figure has been used to give me a good idea of what a human figure fixed in this pose would look like. The cartoon drawing alongside illustrates just how helpful lay figures can be. The cartoon man was first lightly drawn as a

40. A very useful aid.

lay figure which was then developed into the finished ink cartoon character.

Lightly draw in pencil your idea of a cartoon man then ink it in when you are satisfied with your rough. Feel free to change

41. A running pose.

42. Much better than drawing from memory.

the cartoon figure to whatever you want. Male or female. Why not both?

Figure 41 shows my lay figure frozen in a running pose. Note the adjoining cartoon. Draw your version. Don't forget the word balloon. Do the same exercise with figure 42. Figure 43 sets a pose for you to make up a cartoon from.

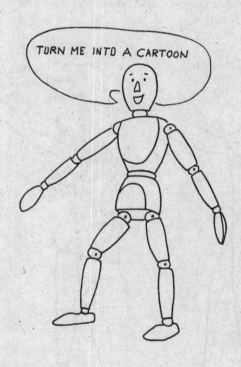

TURN ME INTO A CARTOON

43. A small test for you.

Lay figures are very much better to draw from than photographs or from memory. Raid the housekeeping jar and buy one!

Stick with it

If you are on a tight budget and cannot afford a lay figure do not worry. There is another way to help yourself. Use stick figures to form the basic structure of your cartoon figures. First think about the position you want your cartoon character to be in. Then draw it as a simple stick figure to depict the position you require. Then you carefully pad out the stick into a cartoon form. Figure 44 will show you how this is done. Try this one for practice.

44. Stick lady filled out.

Figure 45 of a tubby cartoon chap was first drawn as a stick figure. It was then bloated out to what was needed. Draw your version of this sketch. Put in a word balloon. Who is this guy? What is he talking about? I'm sure that you can come up with a sparkling one-liner.

45. A stick man bloated out.

To get the hang of drawing figures think about what is involved in the movement of a human. Use yourself as a model. Of course, if you have a lay figure you have a little slave who will do as you want. Isn't that a happy thought? I've been looking around for years for one which would do all the housework, cooking and so forth!

Figure 46 depicts a man walking. Note the body action. Use a lay or stick figure to draw your little chap strutting his stuff.

46.   Walking with purpose.

Assignments
1.   Draw from a lay or stick figure a lady kneeling down.
2.   Using a stick figure draw a cartoon man climbing a ladder.
3.   From my drawings sketch a lay figure jumping up and down.

47.   Little bopper!

6

Lurk Out And About

The art of lurking is a fairly easy one for you to acquire. The top lurkers are undercover police, private detectives, professional master criminals and some cartoonists.

How to lurk
Successful lurking requires acting ability. You need to be furtive without looking as if you are. You must get this bit right otherwise you could well feel some old lady's walking stick across your shoulders as she shrieks 'PERVERT' with the power of a fog horn. This wouldn't be nice but might provide a good gag after you have escaped the hostile crowd who would quickly gather.

The trick is to appear to be doing something quite different from your undercover cartooning of various victims. You could, for instance, sit in your car and appear to be totally bewildered by something whilst you craftily jot down the passers-by who will most certainly ignore you. If you happen to be on foot, a safe bet is to pretend to scan the sky for a possible sudden change in the weather, UFO or unseen high-flying bird. When everyone is looking up you glance down and deftly pencil a few rough cartoons.

My favourite ploy is to sit either inside or outside a cafe, enjoy a drink and gaze about like a short sighted person or one who is quite dotty, blighted with a nervous twitch with a tendency to go cross-eyed from time to time. You then

48. Drawn from my car.

become embarrassing to look at. This never fails. People do not come near you. They never notice the sketch pad on your knee or hidden amongst the plates of cake.

Drawing from the inside of a car works very well. People can't see what you are doing when you look down at your sketch. Figure 48 is a cartoon which was produced this way. Figure 49 showing two ladies having a chat was another one.

49. A conversation spotted from my car.

Study the help lines then sketch your versions of these two cartoons.

Try quickly jotting down figures whilst you are watching TV.
You will soon get the hang of doing this with practice and it
will provide you with dozens of cartoon figures.

50.   A golf fan seen on TV.

I watched a live TV golf programme. My eye was caught by
spectators in the background. You can see these in figures 50

and 51. Note the long shorts, shapeless shirts and golf caps. See what you can come up with.

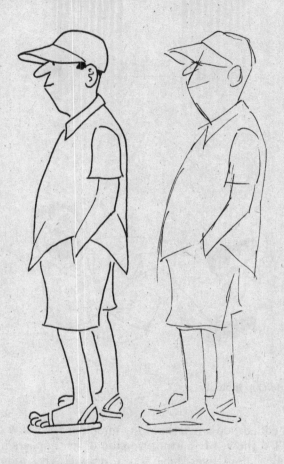

51. Another golf watcher.

Like millions of other folk I watch football matches. It seems to me that far too many professional footballers are unsporting. Some play act being badly hurt, in order to get their opponent sent off (plus a free kick). I caught one of these jokers on my sketch pad. Have a look at figure 52.

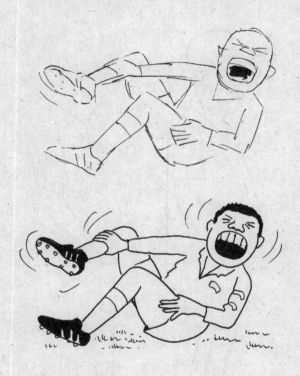

52. World Cup footballer!

A so-called pop singer held my attention for a few minutes on one TV show. My cartoon version of her appears in figure 53. Notice how eyes have been drawn. The mouth was exaggerated. Try drawing another girl singer this way.

Newspapers can help you
If you are housebound or pushed for time, try using your newspaper for creating cartoon characters. Figures 54 and 55

53. Pop singer cartooned.

are my examples of doing this. Notice that the chap in figure
54 is life-like whilst the fellow in figure 55 has been exaggerated a lot. It's up to you how you draw the characters *you*
want. Drawing cartoons from different publications is a good
way quickly to churn out an army of varied characters. You
can sketch figures as you watch TV, carry on talking to friends
or as you simply relax. Give it a try after drawing your
versions of figures 54 and 55. The soap-box orator, figure 56,
requires a word balloon. A small job for you, mate.

54. Quite life-like.

Lurk in your supermarket

A supermarket is a great place for a cartoonist to lurk about in. It's easy to hide away somewhere when there is so much activity going on and with people being occupied with their shopping.

The lady featured in figure 57 represents a species almost always seen out shopping. She is large, cheerful and delighted to be let loose in a supermarket. Note how the tight curls have been drawn by using a controlled scribble. Draw a pencil rough of this figure then ink it in.

Both of my victims used for figure 58 were spotted in a supermarket. The old lady was rushing about at high speed. I wondered how she would be on roller blades. The stout

55. More exaggerated.

56. Soap-box orator.

63

57. There's usually one of these!

58. Converted from supermarket victims.

gentleman was looking for something. He reminded me of a darts player so I drew him as such. These two examples make the point of using *imagination* to create cartoon characters from ordinary victims. The help lines for these cartoons are like most of my first pencil roughs. Try to get into the habit of drawing often. Then you will soon become quick and competent. See how fast you can sketch your versions of my characters.

Assignments
1. Draw a male and female cartoon figure from life.
2. Lurk in a supermarket to draw unsuspecting victims.
3. From TV sketch two original cartoon figures.

59. Gotcha!

7

Cartoon Kids

Drawing cartoons of children is similar to sketching adults. The differences are small. Kids have larger heads, smaller bodies and dress like children. The quickest way of learning how to draw them is to observe carefully, then draw fast pencil roughs. Youngsters tend to move about a lot smarter than us adults. Do not lurk about school gates in order to watch and sketch children or you could be in big trouble. Try to observe your friends' or relatives' children. In any event there are always plenty of kids around during school holidays so finding victims is no real problem.

Capture moods
After drawing examples in previous chapters you should be aware of the facial features which denote moods. But just to refresh your brain I will go over the three most important features to concentrate on.

The mouth line, eyebrows and eyes can all point to the mood of a person. Study figure 60. In this illustration you will see how the faces of a boy and girl have been used to reflect different moods. Look at the top line. The first cartoon shows a surprised expression. Mouth is o-shaped, eyebrows are arched with the pupils centred in a round circle. The middle sketch is of a happy face. Mouth line curves slightly upwards, eyebrows are arched and eyes look normal. The top right face

60. Moods.

expresses a big laugh or great joy. Smiling, open mouth, eyes
shut, eyebrows raised.

Now move down to the second row. The face on the left depicts anger or a lot of irritation. Mouth arches down as do the eyebrows. By drawing the top eyelids angled down the mood is further reinforced. The middle expression is one of neutrality. Here the cartoon character looks as if he does not quite know what's going on. The mouth is straight, eyebrows slightly arched with eyes rather wide. The right hand face shows an up and down mouth line, startled eyes and arched eyebrows. What can this mood be? What if this little lad was feeling completely baffled? This might suggest just that.

The girl, left, third row down, appears to be rather doubtful about something. Notice that she is looking out of the corner of her eyes. Her mouth is just slightly down. No eyebrows are visible. The middle expression reveals a little worried look. Mouth down, eyes upwards and looking right. The end drawing shows a big smile along with screwed up eyes. She might look like this if she is very pleased or if she is gloating a bit.

Move to the bottom row of faces. The girl's face on the left depicts dismay or irritation. The middle face reveals happiness coupled with a laugh. The right hand face shows pleasure.

There are, of course, a hundred other expressions, some obvious but many are very subtle. Only through practice will you be able to jot down exactly which mood, feeling or emotion your cartoon character has. To begin with simply use obvious moods such as those illustrated in figure 60.

Copy the moods drawn but try to install them in cartoon faces which you have invented.

Watch the little perishers
It is a good idea to take time to watch children. See how they react to each other. Ask yourself what they are up to. Wonder what they are thinking, feeling, expressing or appearing to do.

· Figure 61 is my cartoon drawing of two youngsters who are trying to scare each other but also appear to worry about themselves should their bluff topple over into a bit of a fight. Use a lay figure, or the help lines, to draw these two lads

61. Wanna fight?

actually trying to thump each other whilst worrying about getting hurt. Use thought balloons if necessary.

A small toddler escaping from his mother prompted the

62. **Liberty at last!**

cartoon drawing for figure 62. I simply had the tiny tot speaking to another kid who gives him moral support. Notice how the expressions have been drawn. Draw your version of two small children in a similar scene.

Keep your ears open
When we get older we mix with adults and tend not to listen too much to children. But as a cartoonist, you should make an

63. A little light banter.   **64. What on earth are they saying?**

71

effort to record mentally what children say. Listen to different age groups communicating with each other. It might be a mind opener for you!

Figure 63 illustrates typical banter between a boy and girl. The battle of the sexes starts early nowadays!

Use a lay figure or the help lines to create your own version

65. Freed from school.   66. Battle of the sexes.

of this picture. Think out different words and thoughts which suggest an early impending battle. When you have done this look at figures 64, 65 and 66 to repeat the exercise.

Action kids

As mentioned previously kids are more active than most adults. Let's hope that sport comes to play a bigger part in school timetables – without which we wouldn't have future sporting heroes in the multi-million pound earning bracket.

Figures 67, 68, 69 and 70 depict children setting about

67. Football crazy!

different sporting activities. Notice how the action has been frozen. Learn to use action lines, expressions and exaggeration of some movements. Draw your versions of all these cartoons but create your own little people. Then take a break. Have a

68. Ball play.

glass of plonk, mug of tea or a wander round the shopping centre.

Assignments

1. Draw a boy and girl who actually like each other. Use word or thought balloons.

69. This one is gonna FLY!

70. **Exaggerate the faces.**

2. Draw a cartoon showing a little kid looking petrified.
3. Make a funny sketch of two kids playing a sport not illustrated in this chapter.

71. It's gone!

8

Watch The Birdie

In this chapter you are about to have a break from cartooning
humans. How have you got on with birds up to now, the
feathered sort? You feed them now and again? Good. Bird
watching could help you to become a good animal cartoonist.
You may even earn money with this skill. In any event it's
good clean fun.

Cartooning birds requires the same drawing abilities needed
for sketching human animals. You have to learn how a bird is
put together. This is not hard as most birds have roughly the
same bits and pieces. If you think of a bird's head as being
round or oval and the body the same you will be on the right
track for all birds.

Human-like birds
You have a lot of freedom when you cartoon animals. You can
give them human strengths and weaknesses, have them talk,
think or even wear clothes.

Figure 72 is based very loosely on a thrush. You may have
seen these birds stalking your lawn for worms. Notice how
much I have exaggerated this bird. See how the rough sketch
shows a circle for the head transposed on to an oval for the
body. This is a good system with which to start all bird
drawings. Note how wings, wing feathers and tail have been
sketched.

The gliding rook, fig 73, is again exaggerated from the real

72. Loosely based on the thrush.

73. Rook in full glide.

thing. See how I have left white lines to depict wing feathers. Draw your versions of these two funny birds. Think out different word and thought balloons for your creations.

When you are out in the countryside or in a large park make a note of the birds which you see. It won't be wasted effort. In fact, like me, you could become interested in the subject and learn a great deal about birds.

Figure 74 shows a coot, top sketch, and a young sparrow below this. The coot shape is easy to draw, then block in with

74. Think out suitable word balloons.

a brush and black drawing ink. Try drawing a coot then think out a witty thought balloon for it. These birds are usually nervous of humans but can fight fiercely with each other. The young sparrow depicted is in a common position for young birds. It's calling for food. You might have seen such young-sters looking pathetic, fluttering their little wings whilst per-suading their parents to bring food to their ever-open beaks. Draw your own little bird but use a different word balloon.

75. Tawny owl (juvenile, as they say).

Owls are popular. See figure 75 for my cartoon version of a young tawny owl which is our commonest owl. Notice the ruff round the small, round face. The large eyes, small beak, dark marks on the chest. Imagine a much older owl sitting on a branch whilst thinking some profound thoughts. Now draw your invention.

Notice how birds fly. Some soar around on hot air thermals, others battle slowly into head winds, small finches hurtle about in a series of fast swoops. You can use their flying patterns in your sketches. Figure 76 illustrates a bird flapping upwards and another hovering. Notice the use of action lines

76. The flap and the hover.

to suggest movement. See how large, round eyes are effective when popped into bird cartoon faces. See how you make out with these examples.

Use more humour
It makes for good cartoons if you can add in additional humour to a funny-to-look-at drawing. See figure 77 for a good example. This cartoon was produced by my mate Pat who was once my student. She has a flare for cartoons. I like

77. Give your vulture some instruction!

the vulture, called Vernon, which she came up with. Notice the long, bare neck, ruff of feathers at the base, hooked beak and glasses. Vultures rely on superb vision when searching for food. See if you can think out then draw a similar bird but with a different gag.

The parrot in figure 78 is another little gem drawn by Pat.

78. Get the parrot to talk proper.

The joke was a joint effort. Pat created the cartoon then I supplied the idea: a parrot learning how to speak correctly. See if you can come up with a similar joke.

You can draw life-like birds
If you already know your birds you can make life-like cartoons of them. After studying green woodpeckers then

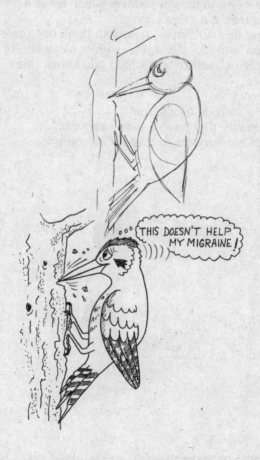

79. **This sort of thing can give you a headache.**

drawing and painting them I used one for the cartoon in figure 79. This pretty little bird is most interesting. Why doesn't it suffer brain damage when it hammers its beak into hard bark? Because its brain is encased in fluid which absorbs the tremendous shock. How does it get insects and grubs from deep inside a tree? It has a very long, sticky tongue which is kept curled round the inside of its skull until it is used. It also has strong stems in the tail feathers which act as a prop when it clings to a tree. Isn't that clever?

Knowing this stuff made it easy to think out a relevant gag. See if you can do the same with a drawing of a green woodpecker or another bird which you know a little about.

Assignments
1. Make a cartoon of a heron.
2. Draw a city pigeon as a funny cartoon.
3. Robins are very much loved. Cartoon one.

80. **Retaliation on the way!**

9

Animal Antics

Animals are often used in cartoons. Any creature can be drawn as a cartoon if, of course, you first observe one carefully. After a little practice and much research you should be able to sketch most animals pretty quickly.

Easy shapes to start with
If you are new to drawing animals, try to begin with creatures which have an easy shape to draw. Figure 81 illustrates two fish. The body shapes are similar, the only real difference is in the mouths. This idea came to me after hearing about an angler who used chocolate as a bait. See if you can think out another gag line for your version of this cartoon.

Sheep are quite easy to sketch. See my rough drawing at the top of figure 82. Notice the oval-shaped body mass and series of small ovals used for head, ears and lower jaw. The hard bit for you might be the legs, so pay extra attention to them. Once you have drawn them a few times you will find that the structure of these limbs will stick in your mind. Send a mental picture of the animal or cartoon to your personal computer. You can then draw from memory any old time. This applies to *all* drawings.

The crab, lower sketch in figure 82, is another example of building up a cartoon from ovals. Draw cartoons of these animals, then see if you can come up with a funny line for a word or thought balloon.

81. Time for a change.

Popular pets

Cats have become the number one pet in the U.K., which comes as no surprise to me as a former keeper of cats. The best way to learn how to draw a cat is to watch one. Look carefully at ears, eyes, nose and skull shape. Once you can put these down, more or less accurately, from then on you should be able to draw a moggie from memory. Look at figure 83. This cartoon is fairly life-like. I find that tatty alley cats prompt the most cartoon ideas for me.

82. All based on ovals.

Draw a page of cats to prove what was previously mentioned about sending pictures to your computer for future use.

The cat featured in figure 84 has been exaggerated a little more than the moggie in figure 83. It has human-like limbs. It stands on two legs. The lower half of the face has been drawn bigger and more rounded than it actually is. You can dress your cat in clothes if you like. This type of cartoon is loved by children.

You must have seen the many cartoon cats made famous by

83. Cats can be very expressive.

years of use in daily newspapers and TV cartoon shows. If you can invent a really new addition, a fortune awaits you. For the time being try out your skill on figures 83 and 84.

Dogs follow cats in the popularity scale. I tend to draw life-like dogs as cartoons, but you can make yours totally comic if you want to. See figure 85 for my version of a basset hound. These animals seem to look worried or unhappy but they are not really. This point is made in the word balloon

84. Try to create an original character!

used. Try your skill on this dog or one you know or may have as a pet.

The cartoon dog in figure 86 is again one which can stand on two legs. Another children's type cartoon invention. Notice how the rough sketch is made up of circles to produce a head, face and body. Draw your own cartoon dog based on my drawing.

Children love rabbits too. See figure 87 for my example. The bulldog below is rather sad-looking. This is life-like with just the eyes, frown lines and mouth exaggerated. What do you reckon these two animals are saying or thinking? Exercise

85. Use a real dog.

your imagination on your drawings of them, then pop in suitable balloons.

86. More of a children's type of cartoon dog.

Feature all creatures

Try your cartooning skills on all animals. The problems are the same for most sketches. First build a good rough, then ink in the finished design. Study the horse in figure 88. The body is a rough oval, the legs are rather straight with flat-iron-like feet. The face is life-like but put this down to my particular style. Don't be afraid to express your own thing. You could easily come up with a funnier cartoon. Draw it now.

A kangaroo is quite comical to look at so it does not require much to draw one as a cartoon. See mine in figure 89. A kangaroo using its pouch for something other than raising youngsters is not an original idea, but a witty thought balloon could give an old gag a new twist. See if you can think of one after you have drawn your cartoon kangaroo.

A camel is a natural cartoon. Since one wretched specimen in France tried to bite my arm off, I am not over-fond of these

87. Discover what children like!

smelly, evil-tempered creatures. Nevertheless they do make good cartoons. Figure 90 shows my idea. See if you can better this one.

My lion drawing in figure 91 resembles a real one apart from the huge eyes put in. Exaggerating the eyes is a sure way of making an animal sketch more cartoon-like. See how the rough sketch has been prepared, then have a go yourself.

88. Cartoon horse.

89. Pop up with a caption.

You must have seen the famous TV commercial chimpanzees swilling back cups of tea. This popular series gave the idea for my cartoon in figure 92. It occurred to me that the poor things might prefer a pint of strong beer for a change.

90.   The camel's hump is an ugly hump.

Draw a cartoon chimp then think out a funny word or thought
balloon to go with it.

91. The king of the jungle.

92.   . . .hic.

Assignments

1. Draw a cartoon of your favourite pet. Put a witty caption in it.
2. Cartoon an elephant.
3. Invent cartoon and thought balloons for two different animals confronting each other.

93. It's a wind-up.

10

Pin Up Your Pin Ups

You are back drawing humans for this chapter. As we all know, pretty girls are used to sell all kinds of goods. The same is true of cartoons. A fetching pin up could make a lot of loot for you. You are about to learn how to draw scantily clad girls. I know this might be a bit of a strain for you, lad, but force yourself!

Use photographs
When you begin to draw pin ups it will help you to use a lay figure or good photographs as a basis. Study figure 94. This model was featured in a glossy magazine. I retained her haughty look but exaggerated the length of her legs. I liked the smooth flowing lines provided by the long dress. A classy look can still be cartooned and yet be pretty life-like. Draw a cartoon based on my sketch but change the face if you want to.

The model in figure 95 is another example of what can be done from a glossy picture. This young lady only needed a cartoon type face added on to a life-like body. This sort of drawing can be used to advertise different products. Notice clothes styles for your models. Try your skill on a similar drawing.

Figure 96 was drawn after I saw a newspaper picture of a Beauty Queen contestant. Legs were lengthened, waist narrowed, hips and bust size increased along with eyes. This shouldn't be too hard for you.

94. **Lovely flowing lines.**

95. Drawn from a photograph.

Invent your pin ups
You can easily invent a pin up type for your cartoons. All you
need is practice, plus the knowledge, listed above, of which

96. Beauty Queen with everything exaggerated.

features to exaggerate. Now see figure 97. Mentally work out which features have been worked on. Note the tarty-looking clothes, large bosom, long legs, short skirt, fish-net stockings.

This kind of pin up is useful for popping in pocket cartoons. There will be more about this sort of cartoon in a later chapter. Draw a girl as in figure 97 then include a word balloon. What could she be saying or thinking? It's up to you, chum.

The idea for the pin up in figure 98 came to me after seeing a very old movie which included a scene about wannabe

97. Tarty look.

98.   Unforgettable face and hairstyle.

Beauty Queens. I quite like the cartoon face created for this one. See if you can invent a similar pin up. Put in a witty or telling thought balloon.

Holiday pin ups
Holidays provide opportunities for sketching pin ups. There are many pretty girls around who wear very little on sunny days. You need to be careful when lurking about beaches, however. If you creep about looking too seedy you could end

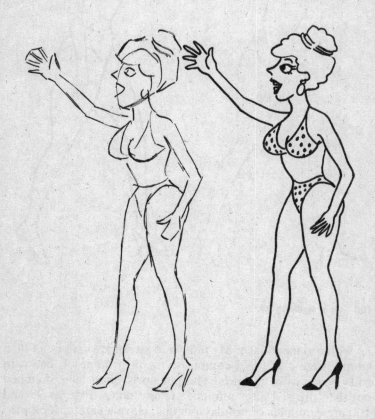

99. Bye bye – see you next year.

100. Just walking by.

up with a slapped face. My ploy is to sit somewhere quiet then
simply gaze about as I commit to memory some of the swim
suits being worn by girls. The pin up is often later sketched
out then dressed after reference to my notes. Figures 99 and
100 are examples of holiday pin ups. Have a careful look then
draw your versions with thought or word balloons.

Figure 101 is based on a sleeping beauty. It is life-like with just the head exaggerated. Sleeping pin ups, of course, are excellent models. See if you can draw a similar one.

Figure 102 has the usual features exaggerated. Re-draw her

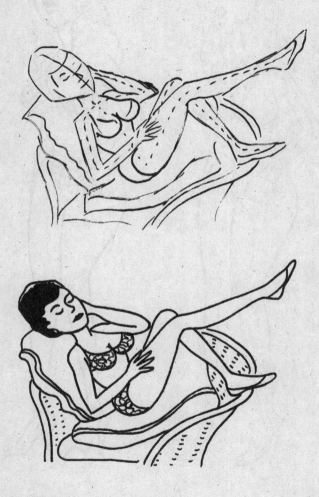

101. Sleeping beauty.

102. Observe swimsuits carefully.

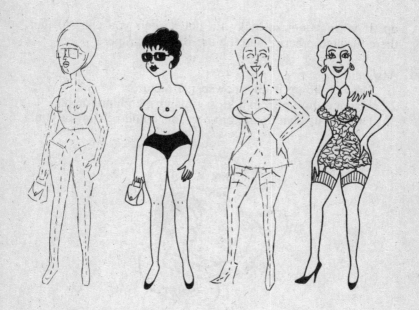

103. Toplessness is all the rage.   104. Exotic underwear.

then add in what she is thinking.

There are many seaside resorts at home and abroad which now have a sprinkling of topless young ladies. I have cartooned an example for you to practise on in figure 103. Mine is life-like; you could make yours much more exaggerated.

Notice undies

In your efforts to draw pin ups try to force yourself to notice fancy underwear used by some glamour girls. It might be safer not to check up on live models. Use photographs, mail order catalogues or furtive research in shop windows. Figure 104 should give you some idea of what is required. See if you can draw a different pin up who is wearing something different from the one illustrated.

It could be that you have a partner or friend who would be willing to pose for you in your quest to produce a unique pin

111

up. If you are not so lucky do not despair you can still get there through practice and the use of photographs.

Assignments
1. Draw a pin up from a newspaper picture.
2. Invent a pin up from a glossy magazine photograph.
3. Draw your own dream pin up. This could be fun for you.

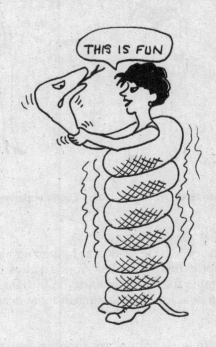

105. Double squeeze.

11

Lots Of Ideas

A major problem most cartoonists encounter is how to think out a steady stream of good cartoon jokes. To a beginner this seems, at first, an impossible task but there is a right way of going about it. In this chapter I will explain what has worked for me and suggest themes which always provide cartoon ideas. How to sell your work will be explained at the end of this book in Chapter 25.

Straight from life is best
For me the very best cartoon gags have come straight from life. The raw material for most cartoons is, of course, people, the things they say and do. By using your eyes and ears you can soon begin to experience the funny side of life from a cartoonist's point of view. An example of this happened to me many years ago when I had just walked past a garage. A motorist drove out onto the road. A front wheel then came off his car. Poor chap. But how funny!

My cartoon of this incident was exaggerated. It was published in a weekly national newspaper. See figure 106. Notice the use of action lines. The background is simply drawn using a few lines.

During the time I took part in rambles with a large, well organised Ramblers' Club there were many funny sights and sayings to feed my cartoon mind.

One incident happened when our group came across a huge

106. "Sold that one just in time!"

tree trunk which had been felled across our Right of Way path. Our leader jumped on the trunk, glared at us and roared: "Which one of you did this?" The good man had a sense of humour.

My cartoon showed a similar scene with the same words. The only difference was a little fellow in the foreground who smiled and held a Swiss Army Penknife behind his back. This cartoon eventually appeared in my first book along with many other rambler jokes.

On another occasion I led a walk and for fun decided to pretend that I couldn't read a map. I pointed to a thin blue line running down the map. "We walk along this track," I told my group. All ramblers know that a stream or river is indicated by a blue line. I later drew this out as a cartoon which was published.

Each of these true incidents which happened along the way made useful cartoons.

Be prepared
When you get into the swing of thinking out cartoon jokes you should find that ideas beget ideas. Sometimes you may wonder where they all come from. This, of course, is great when it happens. Nothing is worse than forgetting good gags because you haven't written them down. Believe me, if you don't do this the idea will escape for ever. Always carry a small note pad and a pencil with you. Keep one by your bedside to capture the jokes which flick through your mind when you should be asleep.

A word of warning about taking idea finding too seriously. Do not worry if at times ideas seem hard to come by. It's a sad

107. "This lot's in The Tate's spring exhibition."

fact that one of the side-effects of constantly producing humour, often under pressure, is to become manic-depressive. This condition has affected many comics, caricaturists and cartoonists.

Use your emotions for laughs

You can often come up with a good cartoon simply by exaggerating something which annoys or worries you. When, for example, I see what London Art Establishments put on show as modern art I feel outraged as do thousands of other normal people. Our feelings, however, are ignored. The weird selectors of new art continue to insult our intelligence. Some of the national newspapers, by the way, endorse my thoughts on displaying awful rubbish as art.

My anger was turned into humour by thinking out then drawing the cartoon in figure 107. This cartoon says it all for me. It's much healthier to turn rage into laughter isn't it? After

108. "Actually, it's the old plumbing from the Gent's loo."

116

109. "I'll just run through how I got my divine hole-in-one . . ."

drawing this cartoon I had another idea based on the same theme. You can see this one in figure 108. Try copying these two cartoons but slightly change your version.

Have you ever been annoyed by someone who was very boring? Yes, of course you have. Now think about turning the experience into a funny gag. A cartoon based on a true life incident prompted the idea shown in figure 109. The same idea was used in a different way for my cartoon depicted in figure 110. Boring people never realise that they are boring!

The sex war for jokes

Strife between partners is a common theme used by cartoonists. There's the hen-pecked husband or put upon wife with many variations to provide dozens of cartoon ideas. The knowledge that some men are lazy is often used by cartoonists. See my gag on this theme in figure 111. Now then, put on your thinking hat and come up with an idea about a lazy wife. Most cartoons about couples can be switched around.

110. "Dear son, just a short note to tell you about . . ."

111. "I HAVE built a rockery. That's it!"

Bring on animals

After finding that gorillas are quite difficult to draw from memory I visited a zoo to practise sketching these wonderful animals. At the same time I tried to think out cartoons which included a gorilla. Some boxers, it seemed to me, are a bit

112. "Don't worry, He's a pussycat."

gorilla-like so I came up with the idea expressed in figure 112. See how the gorilla has been drawn. It had to be like the real thing rather than like a human who resembled it.

Using the same theme I then drew another cartoon showing a gorilla as a goalkeeper. See figure 113. Once more notice how background and other figures have been drawn.

Cartoons about dogs, cats, parrots and other familiar

113. "I like the look of our new goalie!"

animals are popular with editors and readers. You can give your cartoon animals human traits, feelings and reactions. You can have them speak or think so there is a lot of freedom when thinking out animal jokes.

Laughs from sports

Sporting activities provide many cartoons ideas and, of course, appeal to those who take part in a sport. Study newspapers and magazines to find out the sort of jokes used by different editors.

A typical boxing gag is used for figure 114. I'm sure that you can come up with a similar if not better idea on the same theme.

Golf is my hobby. There are often funny incidents which some witty players comment on. Like when I took more than two strokes to get my ball out of a bunker. People can be cruel! Figure 115 illustrates a similar happening.

114. "Brain damaged? He hasn't got a brain!"

115. "He's been in there since yesterday!"

New from old

Years ago during my spell as a freelance cartoonist I met or spoke to several professional cartoonists. We mostly went along the same way when it came to thinking out fresh gags. One system used was called swipe switching. This meant that we swiped each other's ideas but expressed them differently. Ideas are not copyright. Drawings are, however, so we don't copy another artist's drawing, but we can use the idea in a different way.

I recently saw a cartoon which featured a newly married couple sitting in the back of a car. The groom was depicted using the bride's dress to polish his shoes. This gag didn't need a caption. This type of visual joke is highly prized by some editors because if sold abroad no translation is required.

I used the same idea in a different way to illustrate figure 116. I simply took the idea further as you can see. It was a new twist to the same joke. This is a common practice.

116. No caption needed for this one.

One of my cartoons which was swipe switched was about the weather. My drawing showed a weatherman standing before a weather chart. The caption read: "There will be scattered thunderstorms, torrential rain, hail and snow, then in the afternoon the weather becomes worse." I've seen this same idea used several times and also heard it used as a one-liner in a TV show.

Some old jokes go on for years. Do not be afraid to use any idea in a different way. Having stated this, however, I still reckon the very best jokes are those which come straight from life.

Assignments
1. Think out then draw an animal cartoon.
2. Work out a father-in-law joke to draw.
3. Use a funny saying to create a cartoon.

117. Victory!

12

Set About Your Friends

In this chapter you can learn first steps towards caricaturing.
This art form is a continuation of cartooning. The main
difference is that you produce sketches which resemble your
victims.

Start with known victims
The best way to begin is to set about the victims you know
well. Why? Because you already know what they look like
from every angle. Your first aim is to try to get a reasonable
likeness into *cartoons* of your friends and acquaintances. You
should know what your victims work at or do for a hobby.
This will help you to put a bit of humour into your master-
pieces. Don't worry about your victims taking offence when
they set eyes on your gems. Pretty well everybody I've
cartooned or caricatured has been secretly pleased. They know
that I am half mad but harmless!

Figure 118 is of a victim I like. When told that he would
appear in my book he muttered darkly that he hadn't given his
permission to be drawn. I knew that beneath his gruff exterior
lay a heart of gold. He didn't stop me from sketching him,
however, and when presented with a copy of figure 118 he
then announced that his image would be framed. This drawing
is cartoon-like but nevertheless resembles the real person. Do
you know someone like this to work on? See if you can work

118. Choose a good victim.

out help lines to draw your version of my victim. Then have a go at one of your own friends.

My next victim is a lady who I met after she had been on a mini shopping spree. She is not a shopoholic, indeed, she

119.   What does your victim like doing?

devotes many hours of her life to helping others. My cartoon
of her simply reflects one of the things she appears to like
doing. The sketch does faintly resemble her. See if you can
draw someone you know in a similar fashion.

The lady featured in figure 120 is one of those nice people
you cannot help liking. She greets me with the magic words:
''Tea or coffee, luv?'' She also allows me a free run of her

120. I actually like most of my victims.

large, beautiful garden. Friends are wonderful aren't they? This drawing is a step nearer to caricature. I have exaggerated the head size but still retained a cartoon-like drawing. Draw your idea of a nice friend or re-draw a cartoon of my chum.

One of my close friends is quite remarkable. He has one arm but is more capable with one hand than most of us are with two. He made then installed a superb built-in cupboard for me. I rammed it full of art stuff and various bric-a-brac which had previously cluttered up my hovel. I would have

121. A quite remarkable fellow.

great difficulty in knocking together a wooden cross but my pal can do anything. Take a squint at figure 121. Notice how I have increased his head in size to make this sketch a true caricature which is still pretty life-like. See if you can draw him or somebody you know well as a caricature.

Save good photographs

This is the first picture in the book done by the talented caricaturist Colin Henderson, based on one of the many photographs around in the early 2000s of rising tennis star Andy Murray. See how the head is disproportionately large, as in almost all good caricatures, and it doesn't matter in figure

122. Tennis star!

122 that the head of the racquet is very small, or that there are too few strings! Help lines show how he got this one right!

My next victims are people I have come to know but have never met. The folks who toil on their working days for us authors. Just as publishers need authors, authors in turn depend on publishers and their staff. It's a nice partnership, but I could be stamping on dangerous ground. Some of us eccentrics like to take a chance!

Figure 123 is my drawing of a gentleman who is keen on amateur dramatics when not engaged in the book distribution processes. By changing one of Shakespeare's immortal words,

123. Costume better than memory!

discontent, a bit of humour has been added to the drawing. I hope!

Another member of the publishing staff is also interested in amateur dramatics and singing. You can see how she is depicted in figure 124. Do you know anyone who warbles? What about yourself when in a bath? See what you can come up with.

The young lady featured in figure 125 is a keen tennis fan when not promoting books. See how her hair has been drawn. Note the use of action lines. Draw a similar caricature of someone you know who might play tennis or another sport.

124. Do you know anyone who can warble?

POW

125. Keen tennis fan.

A young Learner Driver is my victim for figure 126. See how the Formula One racing car has been sketched. The young man's head has been greatly enlarged. Something you commonly do when caricaturing. Do you know anyone who

126. Vroom vroom!

would like a spin in such a fast car? Draw a similar cartoon but put a friend at the wheel just for fun. The youngster in figure 127 is a football fan. I'm sure you must know one of these who you can caricature.

127. Soccer mad.

My final caricature in this chapter is figure 128. I'm really pushing my luck with this one. It features the bosses of Clarion Publishers.

If you have a boss, turn your drawing skill loose. Have fun.

Assignments
1. Look at Super Doodle, figure 129. Continue the series with your ideas and drawings.

128.   The Godfathers.

2.   Cartoon a close friend.
3.   Caricature someone famous.

129.   Bye bye, Super Doodle!

13

How To Draw Caricatures

The top caricaturists are those whose work you see in national newspapers, magazines and on television. The ability to caricature world famous celebrities, often with just a few telling lines, is a demanding skill. This art form can be learned in easy stages. You will continue to find help-line sketches for many drawings in this book, so take heart.

There are thousands of amateur caricaturists who gain satisfaction (and sometimes money) from drawing caricatures of people they know, meet or see around sometimes, maybe, in football, cricket, or other sports clubs.

In the past cigarette cards were widely used to promote the product via life-like caricatures of famous sportsmen. These have now become collectors' items.

Today the majority of published caricatures are life-like rather than like those produced at the pinnacle of this art.

I was once a member of the happy amateur brigade. My cartoons and caricatures of fellow ramblers led directly to my being asked to write and illustrate a first book. A similar happy experience could come your way.

I have designed the second half of this book to show inexperienced or beginner artists how to become competent caricaturists.

What is a caricature?
A caricature is defined, in my battered dictionary, as a grotesque comically exaggerated representation of a person. Also

as a ridiculously poor imitation or version of a person. I call them victims!

A poor imitation, of course, gives you a lot of freedom. Some of the best caricatures appear to have been drawn by backward children. Several students I once taught could naturally draw people in this sort of style. Quite often pupils amazed themselves by having a kind of built-in skill to make comical sketches of fellow humans.

Drawing from life

When some faces can be rapidly jotted down as grotesque or comical records, it's great fun for the artist. Victims, however, may not be overjoyed. Care is needed when you caricature anyone who is within thumping distance of yourself!

It is easier to produce a caricature from someone you know than to draw a famous person from a one-dimensional photograph. You can walk round your live victim, go in for a close look, chat and have a laugh.

The famous

Famous people are fair game for all caricaturists. Top caricaturists enjoy freedom to express what they, their editor, or boss think of anyone. To begin with, forget about making pictures which carry a message. This will naturally come as you progress.

Way back in British history some kings bribed caricaturists not to draw them. The artists concerned enjoyed great prestige and power.

We have all seen the high and mighty brought to earth by a brilliant cartoon. It can be said that political caricaturists do a darned good job. They all too often depict what most of us think. They highlight scandals, expose sleazy Members of Parliament. Fat Cats of industry have their inflated salaries mocked. Big-headed celebrities are not immune to a little wicked humour.

Be a wild child
If you have a wicked sense of humour and can draw like a child you might well have it made as a future brilliant caricaturist! But before you hit the big time there are a few tricks of the trade to learn. I will take you through simple stages of drawing before unleashing you on the world famous.

14

Ways And Means

In this chapter we will consider ways and means of drawing caricatures. It would be best for you to decide on one system then to stick to that until you have achieved your aim. Right?

Look, look, look
One of the most important qualities required for caricaturing is sound observation. Good observation is essential to all forms of art. You cannot draw anything if you are unable to see what shape or form your object is. If, for example, you want to draw a caricature of someone who is blessed with big ears, a crooked mouth, receding hairline and a broken nose then you have an easy-to-draw victim. On the other hand, a person with no outstanding features is difficult to caricature. The key to success is always in careful observation. That's common sense isn't it?

It's sometimes possible to depict a person's face by exaggerating just one or two features. Try to keep your drawing as simple as you can – and as funny as possible.

Pencil power
No two artists work in the same way. You will soon find what is best for you, but for those who have yet to get into a method, I will explain how *I* go about the job.

I always start with a good old drawing pencil, grade 2B, by scribbling a rough sketch on scrap paper. The object is to obtain a reasonable likeness of a victim's mouth, nose, eyes and eyebrows. When that has been achieved I place the rough drawing under a sheet of tracing paper then, still with a pencil, try to improve upon what has been done. This process is repeated with a face shape and body if required. I sometimes manage to get it right straight off but it usually needs several drawings in order to almost please me.

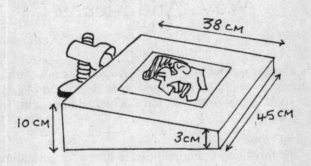

130. A light or viewing box.

When the finished pencil caricature, on tracing paper, is arrived at, it is then transferred to drawing paper. This can be done by rubbing lead pencil on the reverse side of the sketch then using it like carbon paper to make an image onto typing or cartridge paper. The sketch is then ready to be inked in. Pencil marks are erased to leave a finished masterpiece.

A light or viewing box

The best way to transfer pencil work is, however, by using a light box. This is a gadget which can be made or bought. It's simply a box with a sloping top of semi-opaque material such as frosted glass. A small light in the box illuminates the original sketch from underneath. Inking in is then very easy.

My box is made of plastic. It was obtained by post from an art supplies company. Figure 130 will show you what it looks like.

131. Monarch.

The Queen and I

Take a quick look at figure 131. Do you think that my version
of Britain's popular Queen could result in Mark Linley head-
ing the Honours List? Perhaps not. But maybe Her Majesty
will slip a tenner or two my way. Am I being too optimistic?
Oh, well . . .

Notice in my sketch how certain facial features have been
stretched in order to make a humorous portrait. We shall be
returning to this sketch a little later in the book. Then you will
see how a finished caricature is arrived at in easy stages.

Assignments

1. Try tracing any drawing then transferring it to cartridge
   paper.
2. Use the same method to copy the Queen caricature.

15

How To Help Yourself

How can you help yourself to become a good caricaturist? By working through each assignment in this book. The temptation is to skip these but those readers who have a business-like approach have been the ones who have made the quickest progress.

Study as many newspaper and magazine caricatures as you can get hold of. Include funny cartoon characters because caricaturing is simply the next stage. Copy those which you like then re-draw them in your own style or way. By this I mean put a bit of yourself into what you create. Remember that most beginners are much too hard on themselves so expect a few hiccups to start with but never despair. Enjoy what you do, that is the big secret of most success. You can get there. As your graphic skill improves you can begin to think of relevant details to add to your caricature that will enhance the humour. Look for the story behind *every* face.

Practise

My friend and I, when out and about, look for people who strike us as being good cartoon victims. "That's a good one," we say to each other reaching for our pencils. You can mentally practise each time you set eyes on a fellow human. When you read your newspaper or magazine, pause to think how you could make a comical drawing of people seen in print.

I noticed (during my teaching days) that some beginner

artists were rather shy about making grotesque drawings of the famous but had no such feeling about doing a jokey sketch of their best and most understanding pal. Others were just the opposite. They avoided sketching those they knew but joyfully had a go at famous personalities. It appeared to take different people different ways. I hope that you will tackle anybody in as comical a way as possible.

Bag a good hooter

Some caricaturists begin by first drawing the nose of their victim. This is quite a good starting point and not too hard. I would like you now to make your first venture into your new art form by studying my sketches in figure 132. The life-like

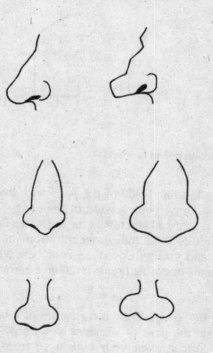

132. Exaggerated noses.

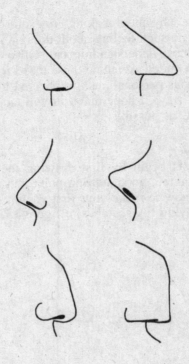

133. Try stretching noses further!

nose is on the left hand side of the page with my caricature of it on the right. Draw your version of the exaggerated noses.

Next go to figure 133 and repeat the exercise. Twenty minutes is the time adults hold their concentration most effectively. Keep to this and you will produce your best work for longer spells. Take a tea or coffee break. You have earned it.

Assignments
1. From a photograph draw a caricature of a nose.
2. Exaggerate the nose of someone you know.
3. Make a caricature of your own nose from the front and side (profile).

16

Slightly Done, Not Burnt!

Now that you have had a little drawing practice on noses you are ready to move on to sketching other facial features. In this chapter you will extend what you did in the last session.

To begin with, concentrate on just slightly exaggerating faces. Think of it as being a bit like cooking. Slightly boil but do not burn to a cinder!

The Big Three

From my own experience I have learnt that in order to obtain a likeness in a face, whether drawn as a straight portrait, cartoon or caricature, it is important to depict the nose, mouth and eyes, including brows, more or less correctly. If this isn't done the drawing will fail.

To show you the importance of accurately drawing the Big Three I have caricatured the face of world famous Hollywood film star Sylvester Stallone. He is the actor who created the fictional character Rambo. The first movie was so successful that follow-ups of the same character were made. Rambo seems to have set a fashion for current film heroes. Many of them now appear to wear tatty vests, grubby headbands and have over-developed arm muscles!

Examine figure 134. See how I have used the heavily hooded eyes, hooked nose, distinctive lips, strong eyebrows, headband, ears and hair style to caricature this wonderful face. Try to copy this illustration for a little advanced practice or wait until I show

147

134. Rambo's face.

you how to add a body on to this face, later on page 170.

Big ears, floppy lugs
You will see, in figure 135, normal ears on the left hand side then slightly exaggerated drawing of these ears on the right of the page. See if you can stretch the examples just a bit further but remember that your caricature ought to resemble the originals.

Some famous people naturally have larger than average ears. Prince Charles is, perhaps, one of the best known examples. This is due to caricaturists depicting the poor man as owning quite enormous lugs. In actual fact the Prince's ears are not all that large. Having stated that, I went along with the crowd by caricaturing Charles in the accepted way. See figure 136. Have a shot at drawing the Prince.

Big trap!
Our faces, as with all our body bits and pieces, vary from those of other humans. It's just as well or we would all be identical clones.

When mouths are drawn from life it is usual for the artist not to draw in each individual tooth. See figure 137. The exception to this rule is when teeth are a definite feature to pick on. Lips are

148

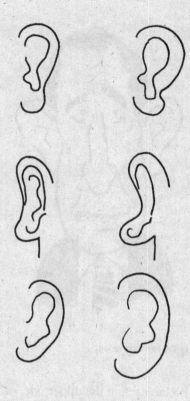

135. Try your hand at ears!

exaggerated in shape and quite often in size. Big mouths are common to caricatures. This is shown in my sketches.

A few famous people were born with larger than normal mouths. Pop star, Mick Jagger is one well-known example. Mouths are a feature to make use of in many caricatures. A mouth can be distinctive when seen from the front or side. Have another look at Rambo, figure 134.

A mouth may be unusual in shape or size. If viewed in profile, it may reveal that the upper lip is much larger than the lower lip. Study the second drawing down in figure 137. A

136. Prince Charles's famous ears.

lower lip could be larger than the upper one, or both lips might stick out a lot. Also revealed will be protruding upper, lower or both sets of teeth. These conditions will always cause a lip or lips to pop forward.

Teeth can be straight, crooked, missing, chipped or gapped. Gums may be hidden when a person smiles, or fully revealed. All these small points should be observed, remembered and roughly sketched in order to produce a well-drawn caricature.

Draw your version of examples in figure 137. Notice how lips can be shaded by using fine lines.

Eyes, brows and nose
To extend what you have now done study the half faces, profile, in figure 138. Once more I have taken normal faces,

150

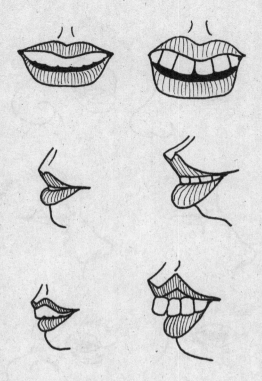

137. Mouths made bigger.

on the left of the illustration, and exaggerated them a little to produce the drawings shown on the right of the page.

Look carefully at them to decide for yourself how much or how little each feature has been used to make a caricature. Ask yourself if noses, for instance, have been shortened, lengthened or made bulbous. What about eyes? Are they drawn larger, smaller or the same. Eyebrows can be a distinctive feature in some people. Think of Charlie Chaplin for example. When brows are very noticeable they are very helpful to the caricaturist. The same is true of eyelids, bags under eyes, and deeply etched face lines. I'm glad that you can't see my mug!

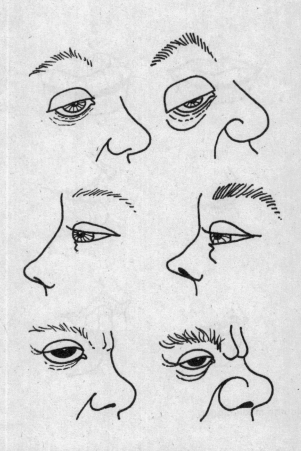

138. Nose, eye and brows, slightly stretched.

Draw your version of my drawings in figure 138 before going on to the next exercise.

Assignments
1. From a photograph draw a mouth in caricature.
2. Draw a caricature mouth, nose and eyes from life.
3. Sketch your own Big Three in caricature form.

17

Fun With Faces

In this chapter you take another small step towards your goal by learning how to caricature whole heads.

Hairy

There are many ways of caricaturing hair. One artist may do the job making hair rather solid looking, another might sketch in just a few wispy strands whilst others seem to scribble in weird shapes and patterns. You should try to evolve what suits you. Study how different caricaturists work.

Have a look at figure 139. Notice, top left, how broken lines have been used to draw a woman's hair. Opposite is a man's thatch, drawn then blocked in. Second one down, left, is another female style but drawn as a series of leaf-like shapes. On the right of this illustration is a Spice Girl type style. This was sketched by using small wavy lines. Third drawing down, left, is a curly haired lady. It was done with controlled scribble made up of little circles. On the right a bearded gentleman. This type of hair is simply drawn as outlines. Bottom left shows a girl's style of short cut produced by solid lines as is the hair on the right. Draw these hair styles as quickly as you can. Why? Because quite often the lightning sketch will produce the best way of caricaturing.

To get an idea of how a hair style suits a particular face I have drawn six examples for figure 140. Can you spot two famous dials? That's right. Baroness Thatcher and that superb

139. Different ways to depict hair.

actor, Sir John Gielgud. Notice how I have exaggerated face shapes in order to make caricatures of the heads. Now test your talent by sketching out your versions of figure 140.

Beards and moustaches are treated the same way as head hair. Some people are natural caricatures. I regard the late actor Buster Merryfield as one of this delightful bunch. He was one of the famous TV cast who created *Only Fools and*

140. Add a face to a hairstyle.

Horses. I have drawn a caricature of Buster by simply exaggerating the magnificent beard he had, then popping legs and
hands sticking out from it. See figure 141. Copy this for fun.

Stretch, flatten, push, or pull
What can a would-be caricaturist do with a face shape? Quite
a lot. A round face, for example, can be made to look like a
perfect circle. A long, thin face could be sketched as a long

141. Buster Merryfield.

strip. Some features can be pulled out: chins, cheeks, foreheads, necks and throats. The same features could also, if required, be pulled in. Once more it's all about looking properly before dashing away with your pencil. Figure 142 illustrates various face shapes which have been stretched a little. Try your hand at these.

One of the best caricaturists, to me, is Gary Smith. His brilliant drawings appear regularly in national newspapers and magazines. He has an enviable talent for using simple shapes to capture the character of whoever he draws. Try to

142. How to stretch faces.

collect then study his work. But remember that there is only one Gary.

Start at the top
To try out my method of working I would like you to draw a caricature of the Queen. This is figure 131 in Chapter 14, but is reproduced here to show the different stages of drawing

143. Above: First rough drawing.
Below: Face roughed in.

which went into it. Study figures 143 and 144. Now use your own style and skill to depict Her Majesty.

If you have already produced the Queen as a caricature turn your attention to Sylvester Stallone and Baroness Thatcher.

Assignments
1. From a photograph draw a whole face as a caricature.
2. Repeat the same exercise on a famous face from the last two chapters.
3. From life draw a whole face caricature.

144. Finished caricature.

18

Get Out!

Without doubt, drawing from life is the quickest way to become a competent artist. The more you can do this the better you will be. Try to discipline yourself to carry a small sketch pad and pencil with you. Then get out to draw the many victims you will come across. Your progress could amaze you!

Work away

I have drawn over twenty people from life in half an hour. The majority of this time was spent just observing my victims. The drawing time per caricature was roughly 30 seconds. You could equal my score easily with a little practice but, to begin with, allow yourself 5 minutes per person.

When you see a possible victim ask yourself which facial features you first notice, what build is the person, what clothes are worn and which characteristics could be used? With practice all this information is taken on board in a few seconds. Then, without further observation, you quickly jot down a first impression.

There are many places which you could visit to further your skill. Shopping centres and malls are super spots to hide away in to observe the human race. Markets and sports meetings also provide good vantage points for caricaturists. Just think about where you go.

Collect faces

Your outdoor experiences should begin with a small collection of faces caricatured. It's good fun drawing these. I have

145. A page of faces.

popped out myself to produce the faces shown in figure 145. Notice how hair has been drawn. My attention was first caught, in fact, by the distinctive hair styles. I made these a feature to

146. Start with rough sketches.

exaggerate. The male victim had a distinctive nose, bless him!

The first rough drawing you make is usually the most important because your finished sketch depends on its accuracy. Sometimes the first impression is the one to use as a caricature. Figure 146 shows how my roughs looked before turning into those in figure 145. Study these drawings before you draw your versions. Try to improve on my sketches.

Figure 147 is the result of catching a very good-to-draw group of victims. They were all so different from each other. Nose, eyes, brows and hats were exaggerated to create the top two

147. Lovely victims!

gentlemen. Face shape, hair style and mouth attracted my attention when drawing the two ladies. See my rough sketches in figure 148 before you turn your talent onto these wonderful faces.

148. The important first impressions.

Assignments
1. Draw a caricature of a lady shopper.
2. Next draw a man shopping.
3. Try to caricature a child.

164

19

Big Head, Small Body

Up to now you have concentrated your efforts on caricaturing faces. Now I want you to add on a body. In my (not too) humble opinion the difference between a cartoon and a caricature is in how the body is depicted. In almost every caricature the head is drawn much larger than the body. In a cartoon the proportions, which may be slightly exaggerated, are more or less to scale. Caricaturists tend to draw little bodies beneath the all important head. The bodies drawn are mostly accurate though miniaturised.

Put a bit of stick about
If you have had little experience of body drawing I suggest that you start by putting a bit of stick about. In other words begin by sketching stick figures which you then thicken out into a proper body shape.

In figure 149 you will see two stick figures. The dotted lines show how the sticks were thickened. This is a very useful trick in obtaining the correct body shape. The people in figure 150, drawn from life, reveal the finished illustration. Copy my stick figures to arrive at the same result.

Look at figure 151 for two more stick figures to work on. The whole bodies are shown in figure 152. These victims were drawn from life. Notice how hair and clothes have been drawn.

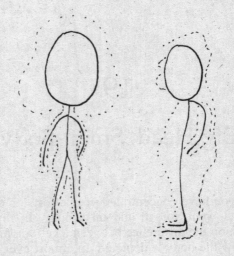

149. Stick figures will help you.

150. Sticks made whole.

166

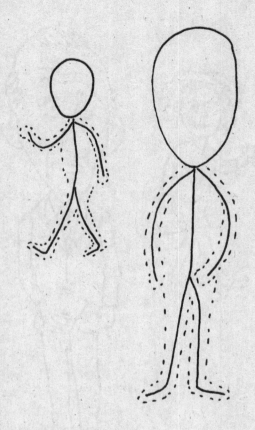

151. More stick figures.

Known victims

As mentioned previously, to begin with it is easier to caricature someone you know. An advantage of using friends as
models is that you can ask them to pose for you briefly. This
may involve you in much funny but useless banter. It's part of
life isn't it? Be prepared for your mate suddenly to become
self-conscious or "camera shy". Use your humour to relax
your victim. "If you don't stop fidgeting about I'll thump

152. The finished drawings.

you," is a line bound to get results!

My victims for figure 153 are chums met on a golf course. One of them, when not playing golf, fishes, or watches football, cricket or boxing on television. I wonder how he manages to arrive on the golf course bright-eyed and fresh

153. **Caricature those you know.**

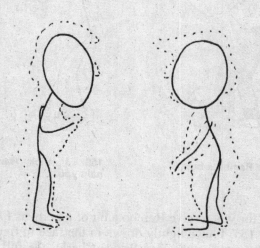

154. **Stick figure help lines.**

enough to beat me. I enjoyed myself exaggerating the figures of my chums. I shall beg for mercy when they see my drawings!

Seriously though, my best sketches of friends have been made when they were not aware of what I was up to. After studying the help lines in figure 154 I should like you to draw a ridiculously poor imitation of the two sporting gents.

Add on

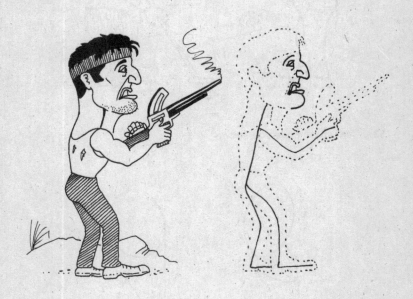

155. **Give Rambo a body!**

156. **A stick Rambo could help you.**

It's time for you to give Rambo a bit of a body as I have done in figure 155. I have lightly drawn in the face in figure 156 to help with your sketch. Give Prince Charles the full treatment as in figures 157 and 158. Finish this section with a caricature of him before taking a break.

157. The full Charlie.

158. A sticky start for Charlie.

Assignments
1. From life draw two caricatures that include the body.
2. After watching children draw caricatures of two of them.
3. Try sketching a rapid caricature of a famous person.

20

Return To School

When caricaturing children you can be quite savage in the way you portray them. Remember how the late great Ronald Searle drew the St Trinians girls? Or how Giles caricatured small babies? A week ago I happened to see a baby who resembled a Giles drawing. Poor little soul. I have to confess, however, to laughing my head off when I drew my version of it. What a sometimes wicked sense of humour I have. See figure 159.

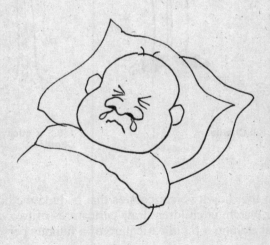

159.   Poor little soul!

Children are a little harder than adults to caricature. They have yet to develop so do not have strong facial features or lines, broken noses, beetling eyebrows and such like. And very few are bald!

Go to school

Now then, if you actually visit a school do not lurk about near it. A large gentleman in a blue suit could feel your collar then take you away for questioning. Would a magistrate believe your innocent plea of just wanting to caricature children? Don't risk it. Ask a head teacher for permission or find a friend who lives opposite to a school as I do! To draw the children featured in figure 160 I went into my front room then watched the little darlings pour out to freedom. I first jotted down a fast impression of two girls waiting for parents to steam up in new cars to carry them a few hundred yards to home and comfort. Will modern children forget how to walk? To help you I have drawn two junior sticks. See figure 161.

Have you noticed how some children wander about with coats not quite on, laces undone, school bags trailing and a general

160. Two small victims.

161. Junior sticks.

appearance of self-induced neglect? All good stuff to us caricaturists. What do you pick on to exaggerate in a child? Try face shape, clothes, build and hair styles (such as there are).

162. Two good subjects.

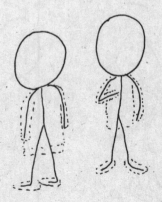

163. First impressions.

164. Draw your version of these children.

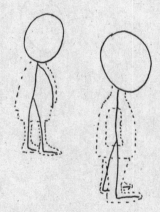

165. More help for you.

To give you a further taste of caricaturing children turn your attention to figure 162 with help for you in figure 163. Figures 164 and 165 will provide a little more practice for you. Notice details like hair, eyes, clothes, expressions and face shapes. You will see that I have not put eyebrows in. The current vogue for hair on some little boys is illustrated in figure 166.

166. Notice details.

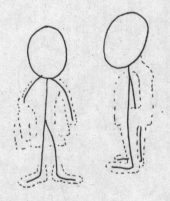

167. Build from here.

Children tend to want their hair done the way their parents'
locks are. Unless the adults are bald of course. Draw your
version of these children after a look at figure 167.

Be fast
It's great fun to dash off quick impressions of children. When
they pour out of school they tend to be hyperactive so a fast,
careful look followed by swift pencil work could give you

168. First impressions can work.

some excellent results. My efforts are shown in figure 168. Notice how I have used shading and a sort of controlled scribble to depict patterns. Draw your version of these children. Start by working out the stick figures.

Assignments
1. From life draw a small child as a caricature.
2. Use your eyes before sketching two older children.
3. Draw a portrait, in caricature, of a child you know.

177

21

Famous Faces

It is now time to let you loose on the famous. There are, of course, hundreds of world famous people. I have selected just a few who are easy to recognise and caricature.

Entertainers
Sir Elton John, colourful entertainer and personality, is known across the world. Look at figure 169, then at the help lines in figure 170, before you draw your version of him. Notice that

169. Draw Sir Elton John.

170. Help lines for Sir.

Sir Elton has a lop-sided mouth and large glasses which make his eyes seem big.

You may have seen Anne Robinson with her gameshow *The Weakest Link*. Doesn't she sometimes seem to go out of

171. **You are the weakest link. Goodbye.**

her way to insult the hapless contestants? Tirade upon tirade of venom is poured upon them until finally they are ejected. She displays sharp wit and acid tongue, but I really don't know why applicants queue up to endure this torture. You should find this face easy to caricature.

Jeremy Clarkson is another popular television personality. For some years he presented the latest, greatest and fastest cars around. He has now moved on to include planes, trains, power boats and all. Doesn't he have a lovely job?

Jeremy's full head of dark, curly hair is a strong feature as

172. Speed merchant.

are his eyebrows. Notice in figure 172 how I have treated the hair. This was drawn in with dozens of little squiggly strokes with a pen. Study the big three features in figure 173 before drawing your masterpiece of this happy guy.

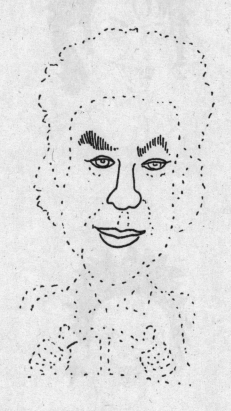

173. Draw the big three accurately.

Another television personality who has come to the fore is that extremely popular American, Ruby Wax, one of very few people whose talents have crossed the Atlantic with conspicuous success. Portrayed here by Colin Henderson, note the

174. Ruby Wax.

175. Help lines for Ruby.

characteristic high cheekbones and hairline, and how this look was developed from the help lines in the lower picture. Don't be afraid to portray black hair as a solid in this way, when the subject suits this treatment.

Which doctor?

Any actor who plays the part of Dr. Who is assured of world-wide coverage and fame. It doesn't seem to matter to the children, and I mean children of any age (!), that the next man to emerge from the *Tardis* may look completely different from the previous one, or that the part has now outlived more than half a dozen actors. David Tennant is one of the more distinguished to occupy this famous role. Have a look at the helplines in figure 177 overleaf, and try your hand to see if you can do better than Colin's effort below!

176. Doctor Who?

177. Helplines for Doctor Who.

In the news

Some folk are frequently in the news. Dozens in fact, but I have selected William Hague, former Tory leader, because he's almost always grinning like a schoolboy. This distinctive face is fine to caricature. See figure 178. I like the small teeth just showing. You might settle on some other feature when you draw William.

Prime Minister's wife, Cherie Blair, is wonderful to caricature. Why? Look at the unusual shape of the lovely lips shown in figure 179. The mouth and lips loosely form a figure of eight on its side. Cherie also has a very distinctive chin line. These two features are enough to caricature. Almost everyone can recognise her from these. See how they show up in the lower help line sketch. Try this. If you get the chin and mouth right you are there.

Like many a serious politician, Gordon Brown is often to be

178. A jolly William Hague.

seen dressed in a suit, and having been one of the longest-serving Chancellors of the Exchequer is well identified by the

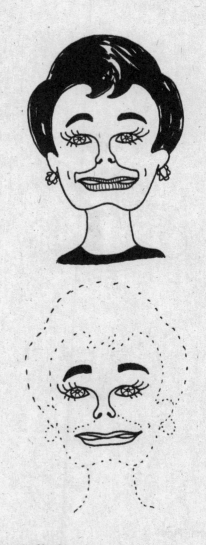

179. Above: Lovely Cherie.
Below: Get the mouth right first.

budget dispatch-box. Have a look at Colin's fine version in figure 180, and consider whether you would do it differently!

180. Gordon Brown.

Assignments
1. Caricature a famous TV star.
2. Turn your talent to a famous film star.
3. Caricature a person in the news.

22

Late Greats

History is littered with late great characters but for this section I have chosen a few of the magic folk who made millions of people laugh and continue to do so years after they died.

Enduring fame

Way back in the roaring twenties three American brothers got together to form a music or vaudeville act. At first it was a tough life for them but then they began to perform in early films. The Marx brothers quickly became world famous. Quite recently I watched one of their old films on television and recalled seeing it as a small child. That's what I call enduring fame.

Groucho Marx outlasted the other brothers to spread his wit through radio, TV and newspapers.

He was a living caricature when attired in his stage gear. He wore a black frock coat, pin-stripe trousers and invented a way of walking with body bent forward from the waist. In one hand, or in his mouth, there was a huge cigar. So here is an easy subject for you to caricature. See figure 181 before grabbing your pencil.

A lovely double act

Shortly after first glimpsing the Marx brothers in movies, I and hundreds of other local kids watched Laurel and Hardy's antics. The children's show was on a Saturday morning. It was

181. Groucho – a natural caricature.

commonly known as the Saturday crush.

Stan Laurel was born in Ulverston, Lancashire in 1895. The house in which he was born is open to the public. When I visited it and saw the gloomy, poverty-stricken environment it is in I could picture young Stanley trying to earn a penny or two by trying to be funny in local clubs and pubs.

His partner, Oliver Hardy, was teamed up with Stanley during early silent film days in Hollywood. Their brand of humour included much destruction, chaos and woe through which their child-like innocent reactions shone, then eventually triumphed. Their old films are still shown all over the world. Unlike a good many performers they were sweet natured and admired each other's work.

Oliver was the one who appeared to be neat and tidy. He was forever trying to smarten his pal Stan up. I have drawn them for figure 182. See the lower sketch for help lines.

The first great comic
Charlie Chaplin struggled through appalling poverty in his early years to become astonishingly famous and wealthy as a comical hero of silent films. Before talkies came in, he had become a millionaire. It was his original comedy plus the advent of movies which catapulted him to world fame in a comparatively short time.

He went on to make sound films some of which he wrote, produced, directed and starred in. What a little bundle of extraordinary talent he was. His standard props were a cane, bowler hat, baggy trousers and black jacket. He was another living caricature. When you draw him you can depict him simply by sketching his eyebrows, nose, moustache, cane and bowler hat. Figures 183 and 184 should put you on the right track.

A legendary lady
Mae West was an artist of the Chaplin era. She performed into old age and was an icon of Hollywood. Where would we be without her immortal lines: ''Come up and see me sometime''

190

182. Above: The immortal Laurel and Hardy.
Below: Help lines for Stan and Oliver.

183. Talented Charlie.

184. Basic lines for Charlie.

or "Peel me a grape"? Her name found its way into the English language after the Air Sea Rescue Service, in World War II, named a life jacket a Mae West. Mae often wore huge wigs for her stage act. I have used this prop in the caricature in figure 185. The stick figure in figure 186 should help you to sketch your version of this past star.

Home-grown late greats

Not many comedians have a sort of built-in ability to make people spontaneously laugh. Big Tommy Cooper, however, was one man with this magic. Tall, with huge flat feet, he had only to walk on stage and stare in bewilderment at his audience to have them falling about. I once spotted him driving round a city centre. He looked absolutely lost and

192

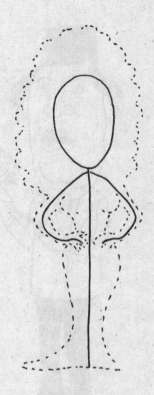

185. Dear old Mae West.

186. Mae as a stick figure.

puzzled. Made me laugh straight off!

His act mostly consisted of performing conjuring tricks which went wrong while he told rather corny jokes. It seemed to be his appearance, the way that he moved, chuckled and his general air of vulnerability which gained the love of his millions of fans.

Study figure 187. Tommy always wore a fez for his act. I exaggerated his look of horror, feet and face shape for this caricature. Figure 188 is your help line sketch. See what you can do. Then take a tea break.

187. Just like that!

188. Help lines for Tommy.

Tony Hancock was another home-grown late great comic. Few performers were good enough to stop the nation's normal life so that over twenty million people could listen to a radio show, but Tony did just that with *Hancock's Half-hour*. He then followed radio success with television fame. He had two brilliant writers in Galton and Simpson plus a superb cast of fellow artistes. Insecurity and alcohol, however, caused him to

189. Troubled Tony.

abandon his supporting actors Sid James, Kenneth Williams and others. His brilliant script-writers were also given the push. What a great shame.

Figure 189 is my caricature of Tony. For this I exaggerated his mouth, nose and heavily-lidded eyes. Figure 190 should help you to caricature this great comic.

190. Help lines for Hancock.

The King
My caricature of Elvis Presley is featured in figure 191. The late lamented Elvis Presley was, of course, the king of rock

191. Elvis the Pelvis.

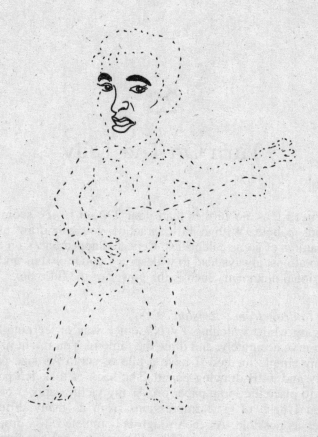

192. Help for the King.

and roll. His powerful voice is still heard on the radio almost every day. A really great late. Figure 192 should help you to caricature this legendary star.

Assignments
1. Caricature a famous late great entertainer.
2. Look back in history to caricature a past historic person.
3. Caricature a past sportsman or sportswoman.

23

Turn On The Telly

You need look no further than your TV set to see scores of famous people. With a little practice you can draw quick caricatures of some celebrities. Repeated appearances on television almost always lead to widespread fame for stars and the occasional unknown. Such is the power of the little box.

How to draw from television
Drawing whilst watching TV is a quick way of learning how to observe accurately, and draw the famous. You might like to try my simple method. I have a pile of scrap A5 size paper handy and a 2B drawing pencil. The back of a sketch pad is used to place the scrap paper on. As my victims appear on the screen I dash off fast impressions from as many different angles as possible. As each rough is completed it is dropped on the floor near my chair. When the programme has finished I then sort through the roughs. The best are re-drawn again before selecting a final one to transfer and ink in. You will be surprised how effective this system is after just a little practice. Sometimes one of your roughs will be good enough to use as it is. There are several examples of first roughs in this and other chapters.

Television presenters
Millionaire television and radio presenter Chris Evans is featured in figure 193. This caricature was drawn from

193.   Presenter Chris Evans.

194.   The big three for Chris.

television. It was my first rough sketch, but captured what I wanted, so was used this way. The teeth, mouth, glasses and eyebrows were first sketched in. The hair was done with a loose scribble-like effect. Figure 194 shows the Big Three. In quick time draw your version of Mr Evans.

Another well-known presenter – and all-round entertainer – is Rolf Harris. His appearances on *Animal Hospital* have increased his fame and fans. Some years ago I happened to see him demonstrate big brush painting. I drew a quick caricature of him. For the one in figure 195 I just jotted down the

195. Good old Rolf Harris.

important lines whilst watching him on a television screen. Figure 196 shows a different treatment of the same subject, by Colin. Which one do you prefer?

Figure 197 is another caricature drawn from a TV programme. This is a good example of fast, loose sketching which comes off. It could be in the mode of "a poor imitation" which is one description of a caricature. What do you think? See figure 198 for the basic construction lines. Sir David Attenborough, of course, is known all over the world. If you draw his mouth, nose and eyes more or less correctly then

196.   A few years later, Colin's view of a more mature Rolf.

197. Sir David and friends.

198. Help lines for Sir David.

your caricature should be fine. Here again we see the addition of other characters that can enhance and finish off your comic creation. Lou and Andy sprang to prominence with their often very rude show *Little Britain*. Well, here they are as seen by Colin. With their distinctive looks you couldn't miss 'em.

199. Little Britons.

200. Good old Brucie!

Bruce Forsyth has been on our TV screens for decades. He has a face which is known the world over and is fairly easy to caricature. For figure 200 I exaggerated his chin, teeth, nose and eyes. Look at figure 201 before making your caricature of this star.

Popular with kiddies of all ages, as well as their grand-parents, Ant and Dec's characteristic Geordie accents back all

201.   Note the distinctive nose!

kinds of quiz and game shows, and figure 202 overleaf shows
them as they are seen by Colin. Helplines in figure 203.

Most mornings whilst at breakfast I listen to popular radio
DJ Terry Wogan's bright and funny show. I became one of his
millions of fans during his first radio programmes on Radio 2
many years ago. Listeners enjoy his quick wit, other listeners'
humorous letters and the general cheerfulness of this show.

202. Ant and Dec.

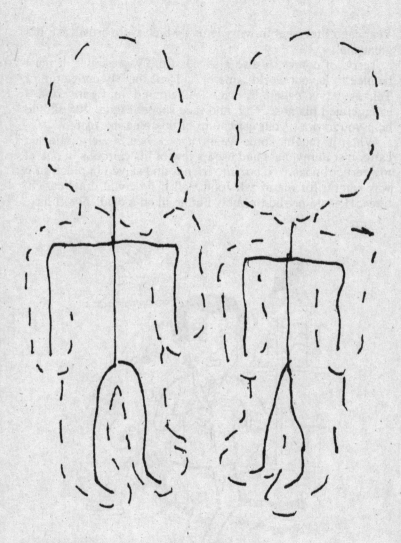

203.   Helplines for Ant and Dec.

Years ago I too sent in witty letters which were broadcast. It's great fun.

Terry, of course, is also a successful TV presenter. It must be nice to have a world fame in both media. My caricature of Tel, as he is called by fans, is featured in figure 204. I exaggerated his nose, chin and face shape. Figure 205 should help you to draw your caricature of this pleasant man.

When I taught some years ago I had a very talented cartoonist in my class and used a few of his cartoons in one of my earlier books. We became friends and stayed in touch so it was natural for me to ask John Ball if he could draw caricatures. He said he didn't know but he liked a challenge. I have

204. Wogan in the bowels of Broadcasting House.

205. Help with Terry Wogan.

great pleasure in using his drawings within these pages. How many other folks are out there with hidden talents?

TV host Michael Parkinson has returned to present a series of chat shows which draw huge audiences. John Ball has captured Parky interviewing. See figure 206. The stick figure is in figure 207.

All in the family
Whether or not Ozzy and the others are your cup of tea, there's no denying that the Osbourne family make perfect subjects for caricature. Colin captures them here using dark shading,

206. Parky interviewing.

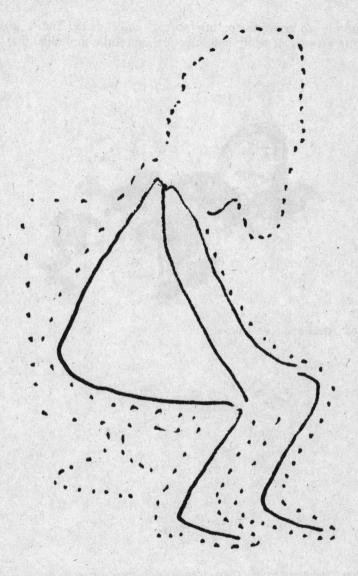

207.   Help lines for the sitting position.

entirely appropriate for this sort of subject, and figure 209 shows a way of using helplines for a multiple topic like this.

208. Ozzy and his relations.

209. Helplines for the Osbournes.

Class

Take a look at figure 210 to see John's caricature of class opera singer Luciano Pavarotti who first came to our notice through televised concerts.

210. Lucky Luciano.

Notice how John has used a bit more humour by sketching in an exploding button. Little things count in this game. John produces his finished drawing by first lightly sketching several pencil roughs on thin layout paper before transferring the final result onto cartridge paper. He uses a dip pen which he combines with a fine-line drawing pen of the sort I use. Look at my help lines in figure 211 before you draw your version of this famous singer.

211.   The basic lines.

Television always needs good writers. One outstanding TV writer is John Mortimer who brought the joys of *Rumpole of the Bailey* to our screens. My friend John is responsible for the excellent caricature of Mr Mortimer in figure 212. Notice the props John has used to fill in the background. If you would like a challenge try to draw your version of this writer by first planning the construction lines.

212. TV writer at work!

Television brought actor, comic, writer, producer and director John Cleese world fame. You may remember his outstanding performances as Basil Fawlty in *Fawlty Towers* which proved to be his springboard to huge success in films. To caricature big John, I exaggerated his chin, eyebrows and face length. One of the supporting actors in the series was Andrew Sachs who played the hapless waiter Manuel. My caricature of

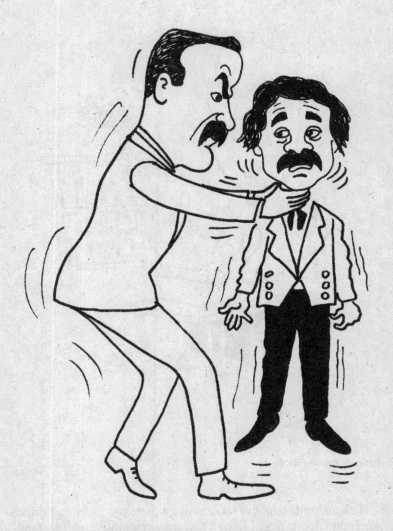

213. Basil (John Cleese) with Manuel (Andrew Sachs).

Manuel is included in figure 213. Glance at the stick figures opposite before you set to work.

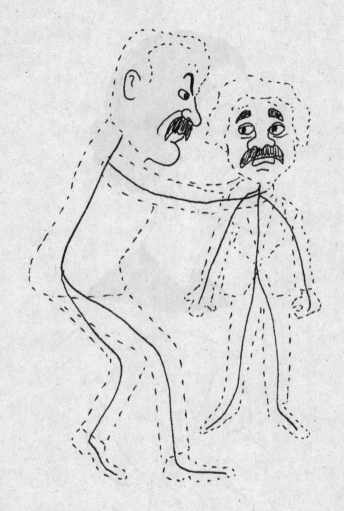

214. The basic lines.

Down at the farm
Emmerdale became one of the best loved of the TV 'soaps',
and the next two pages show my versions of two of its

215. Lorraine Chase.

216. Patsy Kensit.

most popular female stars. Figure 215 depicts Lorraine Chase, the wicked witch of *Emmerdale*. Figure 216 is of Patsy Kensit, who played Sadie in *Emmerdale*, and later starred in another soap, *Holby City*.

One of the most popular sit-coms is *Last of the Summer Wine*. The TV series has run for many years. One of the

217.   Bill Owen (Compo) at the wrong end of Nora Batty's broom.

enduring characters of this comedy is Compo, played by the late Bill Owen. This is another caricature by John. It is shown in figure 217. Notice the use of action lines. Figure 218 will help you to draw your version of this famous star.

218. Basic lines.

219.   Wisecracking Paul and Ian.

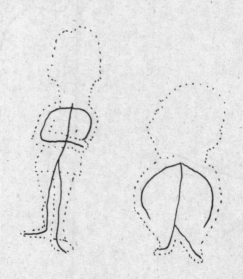

220.   Sticks to help you.

John has featured two popular TV personalities for his caricature used in figure 219. Paul Merton and Ian Hislop regularly appear in *Have I Got News for You*. Paul also stars in his own comedy series. Notice how effectively John has portrayed the short figure of Ian. Figure 220 gives a bit of help with this one.

221. Jasper Carrott Holmes.

Birmingham comic Jasper Carrott enjoys enormous fame for his stand-up performances, but he also starred in the TV series *The Detectives*, so John depicts him here with a

222. Wossy.

Holmesian magnifying glass to make the point.

TV presenter Jonathan Ross, said to be one of the highest paid performers in Britain, may please, or infuriate, according to your point of view. Colin's splendid over-the-top rendition of Wossy in figure 222 brings to an end our gallery of television performers.

Sir John Gielgud, while not strictly a TV actor, became world famous for film and stage roles. A superb all-rounder depicted by John for figure 223. See how shading has been used. See figure 224 for basic lines.

Assignments
1. Watch a TV presenter then quickly caricature the victim.
2. Choose a female TV star to caricature.
3. Study a male TV performer before caricaturing him.

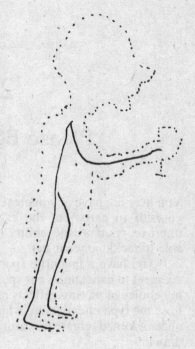

223. Sir John.

224. An easy figure to draw.

24

Please Be A Sport

You may not have any interest in sport. If this is so try to force yourself to carry out the exercises in this chapter. It will improve your artistic ability. A good caricaturist should be able to tackle any subject.

If you have a favourite sport you will not need my encouragement to caricature your sporting heroes. I'm no different so my choice of victims reflects my interests. For sporting figures I use the type of caricature which is seen in pubs and clubs and once adorned cigarette cards. This is my natural style of drawing.

Fore!

I have had the pleasure of seeing top European Championship golfer Colin Montgomerie in action during a few major tournaments. I was too absorbed in the super golf to draw but remember Colin's grim determination to win. I have tried to capture this mood in my sketch for figure 225. I exaggerated his sturdy build, mop of curly hair and nose.

Monty, as he is popularly known, is a superb player. Watching him play was an education. He is able to hit a golf ball a huge distance to land a few feet from the hole. I can't understand why so many of my golf shots hit trees, end up in deep sand or knee-length grass. It's a tough game!

Figure 226 will show you the help lines for this caricature.

225.   Monty in action.

Notice how to capture action by first getting the stick figure right.

When you draw sportsmen or women you learn about the equipment used, mode of action, clothes and so on.

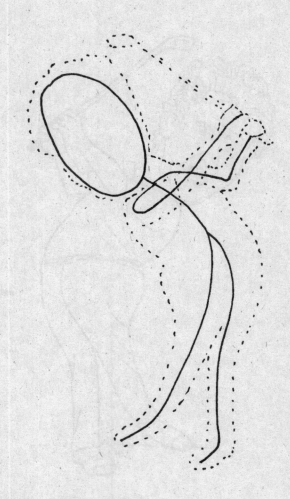

226. Help lines for this big man.

A sensational golfer

When young Tiger Woods became a professional golfer in 1997 he broke nine world records and earned more money than any other golfer has in such a short time. The amount has been put at between 30 and 60 million dollars. How would you like that as your first year's salary? You would? Right, rush out for golf lessons!

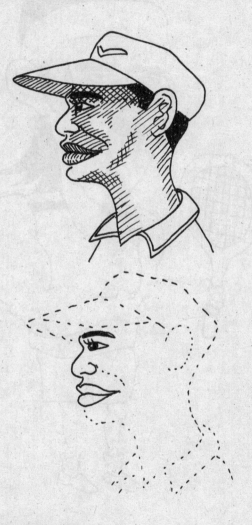

227. Sensational Tiger Woods.

228. Rafael Nadal.

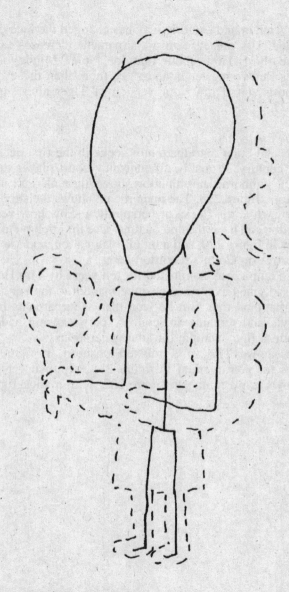

229. This stick figure will help you.

Tiger's talent and exciting play has changed the face of golf worldwide. His presence in a tournament increases fans by over one third. How about that for fame? Mind you, the pressures this youngster is under are more than those of any other sports star. Draw your version of Tiger after studying figure 227.

Everyone for tennis

Rafael Nadal burst onto the tennis scene in the first decade of the 21st century. Probably a better clay court player than on grass, his stubborn determination shows through well in Colin's picture, figure 228. The open mouth shows the strength of character, while the flecks of perspiration show how very hot Wimbledon can be at the end of June. Use the stick picture and helplines in figure 229, add a bit of imagination, and see if you can improve on Colin's rendition here.

British tennis was dominated for ten years by Tim Henman though sadly he never perhaps quite made it to the very top of the international tree. But he won many tournaments in dazzling style and remains an icon of sportsmanship and good behaviour, a fine example for later generations.

Colin shows Tim in a relaxed position in figure 230, helplines for you overleaf in figure 231. My own version of Tim shows him running in figure 232, with a stick figure in figure 233.

230. Tim in relaxed mode.

231. Helplines for Tim.

232. Tim in action.

233. Stick figures help with action figures.

The top man

Pete Sampras was American Number One and World Number One for many years. He hit the ball powerfully and made tennis look easy. His wide smile, strong eyebrows and curly hair should help you to make a quick caricature of him. See figure 234 and figure 235 for the basic construction.

234. Mighty Pete.

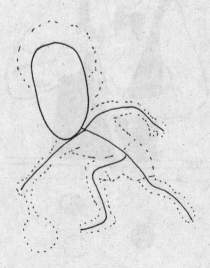

235. Basic structure for the champ!

We each have a hero
Steve Davis is my favourite snooker player. Watching him win snooker tournaments prompted me to try to learn how to play his game. I soon discovered that it wasn't my game.

236. Champion Steve.

Instead of spending a misspent old age in smoke-filled snooker halls I returned to the sport of golf. It was for the best.

Figure 236 depicts my caricature of past world champion Steve who is still pulling in the crowds. He seems a very nice guy. Study the guide lines in figure 237 before you draw him.

It's nice for footballers if they can make a second career as commentators, and few have done that better than Gary

237. **Help with Davis.**

238. Gary Lineker.

Lineker, characterised here in typical style by Colin in figure 238. While on the subject of masters of the dribble and swerve, let us not forget the precocious talent of Wayne

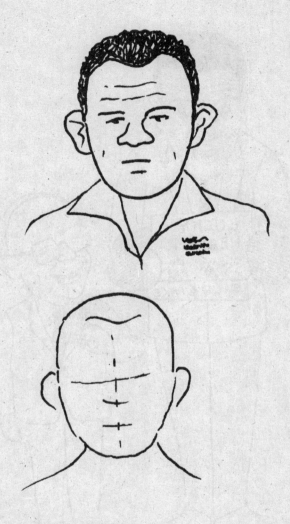

239. Master of dribble and swerve.

Rooney. I have drawn him in very simple style in figure 239, nothing flamboyant but still, I hope, instantly recognisable.

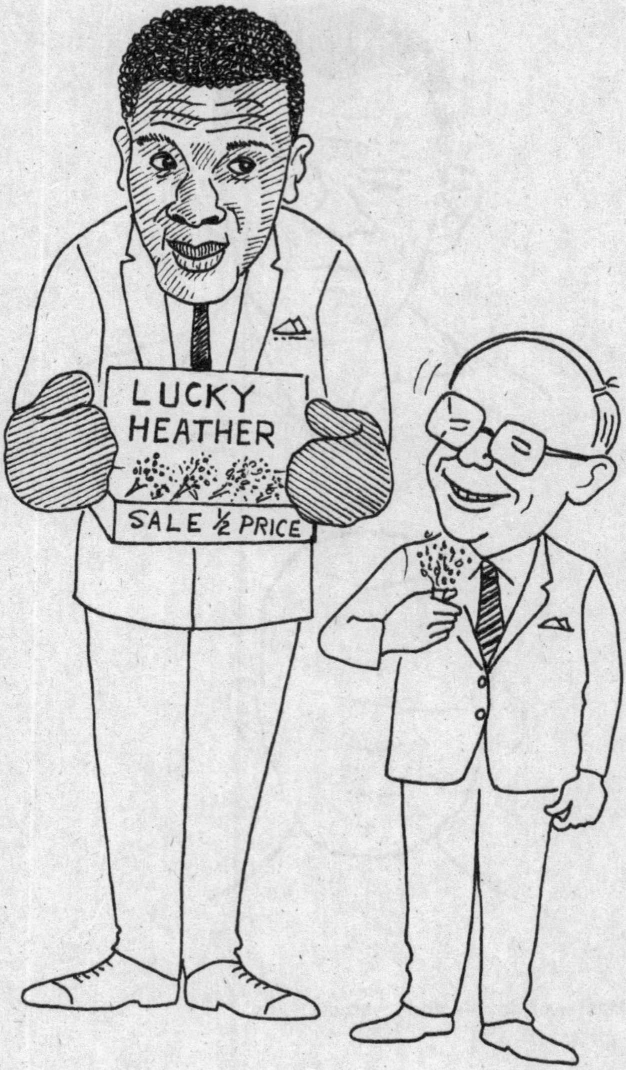
LUCKY
HEATHER
SALE ½ PRICE

240. Know what I mean, Harry?

241. A challenge for you!

Boxing is not one of my favourite sports but I think that big Frank Bruno was a worthy champion who also turned out to shine in the entertainment industry. Know what I mean? A BBC sports commentator sort of linked up with Frank so I have drawn little Harry Carpenter with him for figure 240. See how I have used tiny circles to depict Bruno's hair. Figure 241 should help you to draw a good caricature of this famous pair from yesteryear.

242. Buttoned up!

243. England's goalkeeper.

Easy ones for you
Racing drivers' faces are not perhaps as frequently seen as some – they are too often concealed behind crash helmets as they pound past at 185 m.p.h. But Jason Button has a distinctive look in the flesh; look at Colin's drawing in figure 242. You shouldn't need helplines to draw a caricature of him!

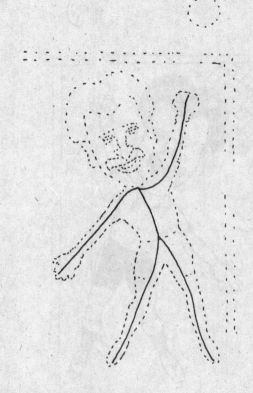

244. David's basic construction.

David Seaman, erstwhile goalkeeper for England is my last choice to represent footballers in this book. He has a very individual hair style, moustache and happy grin which make caricaturing him relatively easy. Take a look at figures 243 and 244 before putting your skill to use.

Assignments
1. Draw a caricature of a famous sportsman.
2. Caricature a famous sportswoman.

25

How To Make Money

The best way of making money with cartoons or caricatures is by starting in your home town. See if your local newspaper ever uses them. They may not have been offered any good ones. Do local organisations such as Residents' Groups or similar organisations need cartoons to advertise themselves? Many outfits, of course, never have the services of an able cartoonist. This is where you step in!

Other possible customers could be large shops, garages and some small businesses. I once used cartoons to advertise a Christmas sale in a toy shop. A garage used my jokes to promote some of their services. Cartoons are a very powerful way of gaining attention, making a selling point and using a simple humour to replace the printed word. Just think how many printed signs you see around every day. Millions of them. A picture is worth a thousand words. Remember that in your sales ploy.

Trade Magazines and Newspapers
Trade publications are another possible outlet for your genius. Years ago I happened across a new magazine which was produced for users of motorised bikes. I wrote to the editor and asked if he would like a few cartoons to brighten up his monthly publication. He did and was delighted with my offer. The fees paid equalled those of national magazines. At that time this was wonderful. I supplied this editor for the short life

of the magazine (mass production of small Japanese motor bikes ended the fad).

You can obtain details of all trade publications from reference books in your library.

It is vital first to read the publications so that you can angle your jokes to what the editor will like. It would be no good, for example, sending mother-in-law gags to a magazine for cat lovers.

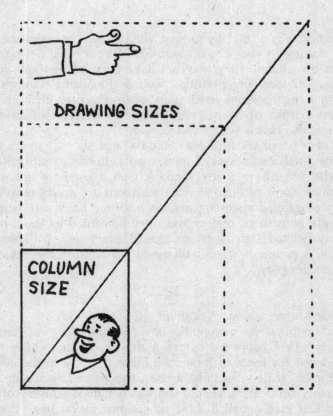

245.   Work out the size.

If you try this route into print remember to send samples of your work, a short, polite letter plus a stamped addressed envelope for the return of your masterpieces.

What size?
Selling cartoons is a serious business. Be professional in the way you go about it. Study your intended customer. Find out what size printed cartoons are. The editor won't consider your work if it's all the wrong size or way normally used by him or her. Many newspapers and magazine editors have original cartoons reduced to fit neatly into a single column. Do not guess at the width and length. Accurately measure, then work out what size you will work to so that your cartoon can easily be reduced to fit into the space your editor has. Figure 245 is to show you how to scale up sizes from a printed single column.

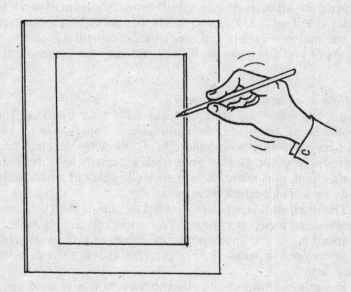

246. Make a frame.

When, by trial and error, you settle on the best size for your original work you should make a simple frame from card as in figure 246. Then each time you want to lay out a cartoon, all you need do is skim a pencil round the inside of the frame. Easy isn't it?

What to draw on

Almost all professional cartoonists draw on good quality typing paper. Good single sheet computer paper works just as well. You buy this sort of paper in reams. A ream is 500 sheets. Why do professionals use typing or similar paper? Because it is a good surface to draw on. To draw hundreds of cartoons in a year on cartridge paper would cost a small fortune. By the way I draw all illustrations for my books on 85g/m (weight) typing paper size A4. I get through two reams per year. Don't be stingy; buy large amounts because it is not expensive. All cartoonists send off a steady stream of work in order to sell just a few cartoons. The pay is high for those used in national newspapers and magazines. You will use up many sheets of paper in your quest for world fame and much loot!

Selling to National Newspapers

After you have had some success with your cartoons you should try to break into the national newspapers. Your jokes will be competing with hundreds of others by different cartoonists. How can you get your work accepted? By sheer hard graft, chum, plus talent and the ability to find out what sort of gags a particular editor most uses.

The usual drill is regularly to send the editor just five or six finished cartoons per time. You must always include a stamped addressed envelope for the return of your work. Buy the envelopes in packs of 25 or even 50. This is cheaper in the long term.

Regardless of rejections you should continue to send out a weekly, or monthly batch of your jokes. One day an editor will recognise that your work is indeed your own, and your own ideas as well. Then the acceptances happen. You are on your way!

How to sell cartoons abroad
When I had been published a few years I decided to try to sell cartoons to American magazines. I was pleasantly surprised to find USA editors treat freelance cartoonists much better than their counterparts in this country. The Americans always wrote to me as if I was doing them a big favour in letting them consider my stuff. How nice! After just one cartoon had been published in a Chicago glossy magazine the editor sent, by

247.   How did you make your first million, sir?

Airmail, six complimentary copies. A little later I received a few letters from readers and a request from an agent (I did not take up this offer). A copy of my first USA published cartoon is in figure 247. Notice that the whole gag is based on what one character is doing. I did not use any background for this one.

If you decide to try your luck abroad always include enough postage for the return of any rejected cartoons. You do this by buying International Reply Coupons from the Post Office to the value of stamps.

You should try to get an idea of what type of gags your editor abroad is interested in before sending off your master-pieces. To sell to another American magazine I used English type jokes because I knew the publication carried advertise-ments by travel companies running trips to the UK. The editor of this magazine accepted a joke about a butler and his Lordship, but it was so long ago I've forgotten what the gag line was!

Do not!

Never include a long letter with your drawings. The editor just will not read it. Do not leave a frame round your cartoon. This would stamp you as a beginner. Do not telephone to discover if work has been accepted. This would get right up an editor's nose! Never use another cartoonist's ideas. Editors have stag-gering memories for old or past jokes. Readers also know which gags have been used.

Do

Be patient. Expect to wait for an answer for two or three weeks. Do use cartoon ideas which are not topical because editors tend to stock-pile cartoons for use. Present attractive-looking finished drawings with the caption carefully printed in capitals. These must be written in pencil only (the editor may change or shorten your caption). It's a good idea to keep a list of where each cartoon has been sent. Put pencilled numbers on the back of every drawing. Do keep on plugging away. You can get there!

Manage yourself

Some beginners try to let someone else sell their work. Do not fall for this. I did years ago and lost a small fortune as a result. I was approached by an agent who had seen my jokes in a national newspaper. He then signed me up along with several other British cartoonists.

This agent was based in Switzerland. He received about two dozen cartoons each month from me. What I didn't then know was that he had many, many copies made of each cartoon then sold them to around 18 different countries. This would have been fine except that I received only a fraction of the money my humour earned. That was bad enough but there was worse. This conman worked with a cartoonist who was talented enough to draw several different styles under several different pen names. Alas, this artist used the best of our ideas to make a fortune. I contacted two well-known cartoonists who confirmed that the same thing appeared to be happening to them. It would have taken years and a lot of money to recover the money lost. At the time I lacked funds so I put the loss down to experience. Let this be a warning to you.

Make money with caricatures as well

Make a modest start. Forget about becoming an instant overnight national caricaturist straight off. This will take loads of practice, talent and a bit of luck.

First get together a good selection of your finished work. Be business-like. Present your gems attractively by using a proper portfolio rather than wrapping in old newspapers. So what's next? Find a customer in your locality. This could be a well-known councillor, or council, a sports personality, maybe local big-shot businessman, publican, or local major or minor celebrity. Try clubs, pubs and any outfit where there are people.

Most people with a sense of humour and normal intelligence are flattered when asked if they could be caricatured. You might try this path to begin with, but don't make the big mistake of drawing for nothing. You are a professional. Charge a small fee or even a payment in kind. I was once paid

248.   Big-shot businessman ballooning.

in Book Tokens for a caricature of a retiring boss.

Your local newspaper may consider your stuff. If it's really good, commissions to caricature local folk could be offered by the editor.

249. An anxious Harry Hill.

Last hints

Keep on drawing. Do not give up if at first you get a caricature wrong. All the drawing you have now done during this course will have increased your powers of observation and accuracy of drawing.

My chum John and I lost count of the number of failed rough sketches we made before managing to obtain a reasonable caricature of some victims. Remember that John had never tried caricaturing until I asked him to have a go.

So, to finish this book, I've used one of his gems, Sir Richard Branson in ballooning mode in figure 248, and finally, one of my own, that anxious comic Harry Hill, at his most worried. Helplines included, but I doubt if you need them any more!

Thank you for being my student. Good luck to you.

250. Throw-away line!